African Initiatives in Christianity

John S. Pobee and Gabriel Ositelu II
Foreword by Walter Hollenweger

African Initiatives in Christianity

The growth, gifts and diversities
of indigenous African churches -
**a challenge to the
ecumenical movement**

Risk
BOOK SERIES

WCC Publications, Geneva

Cover design: Edwin Hassink
Cover photo: Ian Murphy

ISBN 2-8254-1277-5

© 1998 WCC Publications, World Council of Churches,
150 route de Ferney, 1211 Geneva 2, Switzerland

Risk Book Series no. 83

Printed in Switzerland

Table of Contents

Preface

The eighth assembly of the World Council of Churches will be held in Harare, Zimbabwe, in December 1998. This is the second WCC assembly to be held in Africa. The first, in Nairobi in 1975, was an accident – in the sense that the political situation in Indonesia forced a last-minute change of venue. But this one was from the outset meant for Africa.

The eighth assembly is a very significant and critical meeting. It comes in the jubilee year of the WCC – the 50th anniversary of its founding assembly in Amsterdam, and thus at a moment of celebration and stocktaking. This stocktaking takes place at a time when the growing majority of the church worldwide is now in the South, especially Africa, a situation very different from when the WCC assembled in Amsterdam in 1948. And of course this will be the last major WCC meeting in the second millennium of the church and Christianity.

One of the striking features of the changed demography of world Christianity has been the emergence and growth of AICs – African Instituted (or Independent) Churches (we shall turn at once to the issue of terminology in Chapter 1). So, with an assembly approaching in Africa, it was not a surprise that colleagues in the WCC's Offices of Church and Ecumenical Relations and of Communication approached John Pobee to suggest that this phenomenon might be the subject of a book in the Risk series. This is not the first time the Council has shown interest in this topic. Already in 1963 Victor Hayward edited a publication entitled *African Independent Church Movements*. Then in 1971 one of the issues in the earlier Risk series was entitled *...And Some Fell on Good Ground*. Edited by Victor Lamont, it included eight essays, photographs and poems about African Independent Churches. Professor Walter Hollenweger has long been writing about this subject as well.

It was felt that it would be ideal for AICs themselves to write this story, especially now that some of them are members of the WCC. For a number of reasons, however, we were not able to zero in on a single AIC adherent as author. The next best was to get an African, even if not himself of the

AIC tradition, to write in close collaboration with a member of an AIC; and Primate Gabriel Ositelu II, head of the Church of the Lord (Aladura), a member church of the WCC, agreed to work with John Pobee on the manuscript.

We are grateful for the opportunity to introduce AICs to a wider constituency and for this small sign that the WCC is committed to extending the borders of the ecumenical movement in the next millennium. Our gratitude also goes to Professor Hollenweger for not only reading the manuscript but also agreeing to write the foreword to it. We trust that this has been a joyful labour of love for someone who for years has been encouraging WCC staff to take AICs seriously. Finally, we are thankful to Huibert van Beek and Marlin VanElderen for encouraging us to take up this assignment and to Elizabeth Visinand, administrative assistant in the WCC Office of Communication, for putting up with difficult handwriting in typing the whole manuscript.

Rev. Canon J. S. POBEE
Primate GABRIEL OSITELU II

NOTE

We are sorry to report that Primate Ositelu died in April 1998, shortly after finishing his contribution to this book.

Foreword

That Christianity is growing more quickly than the world population is due to the churches in the Third World and in particular to the African Initiatives in Christianity (AICs) and their relatives, the autochthonous Pentecostal churches in many parts of the world. This book, which is the product of a collaboration between Gabriel Ositelu II, a leader in one of the few AICs which is a member of the World Council of Churches, and John Pobee, an African staff member of the WCC, is thus very timely. The centre of gravity of Christianity is shifting to the South – certainly numerically but also, I would suggest, theologically. Ecumenical relationships with these churches are thus becoming more and more important.

The major problem of ecumenical cooperation with these churches is of an organizational nature. The WCC is constituted by churches which belong for the most part to confessional families. But to which confession do AICs belong? Can they be understood as a "confession" or a "denomination"?

It is extremely difficult to place the AICs into a confessional framework. Some look like exotic Anglicans, others like Africanized Pentecostals and still others like evangelicalized Africans, Indians, Koreans, Latin Americans or Indonesians. Common to all is that they do not operate according to the Anglo-Saxon parliamentary system. The combination of strong leadership with democratic participation in a kind of synodal structure of all churches was a stroke of genius by the founders of the WCC. It worked well for quite some time. However, the question is whether this structure is still good enough for the present situation. In an AIC decisions are not taken in a representative synodal structure. Discussions are not conducted in conceptual language (p. 50). The means of communication are not statements but stories, not theological arguments but testimonies, not definitions but participatory dance, not concepts but banquets, not systematic arguments but songs, not hermeneutical analysis but healing.

Western theologians could have learned long ago that these categories have theological dignity. They could have learned this from the Orthodox churches and from the many hymns in the Bible. They could have learned it if they had taken their own research on form-criticism in the New Testament to its conclusion. Still, the question remains: how can such structures be incorporated into the WCC? In the past we banked on "education". In other words: these churches have to become as we are. In this we generously disregarded the fact that *our* theological education and *our* parliamentary system have their snags, both in society and in the church. They produce necessarily discontented minorities (which – due to the representative voting system – are sometimes factual majorities). That the Roman Catholic system with the *present form* of the Petrine ministry is also not ideal is too well known to need further elaboration.[1]

So what is the way forward? I believe that this question can be answered only together with the AICs (and similar churches in the South). There are beginnings of this in the emphasis which recent assemblies of the WCC have given to prayer and worship in many forms of expression. What we have not yet resolved is the translation of these inspirational experiences of unity into written documents (some might question whether this is even possible, but the New Testament is proof that it is). What is a universal expression of the diversity and unity of the church which is congenial to the Christian tradition?[2]

Perhaps a new look at the New Testament could enlighten us. For example, the early Christians did not elect their leaders but chose them by lot. What does this say to us? Conflict management was a highly complex social, liturgical and theological process. Conflicts are generally not solved by majority votes. In New Testament times this went so far that Paul collected an offering for his theological arch-enemies and brought the money, under threats to his life, to the Christians of Jerusalem, the very people who were disturbing his ministry in Galatia. Nor was the eucharist a banquet of those who agreed on every issue. Its very first celebration included zealots (freedom fighters or revolutionaries) and collaborators with the Romans. Christ did not expect them to agree on these issues before they partook in the Lord's supper.[3] There were grave differences between the Hellenistic Jewish Christians which led to open hostility. Nevertheless they stayed together, at least for some time. "There was never a monochrome Christianity" (p. 14).

Perhaps Western theologians can learn from the AICs that elements other than doctrinal conformity are necessary in the struggle for ecumenical unity, that one can be a church leader without understanding the Nicene Creed (p. 41), that denominations based on theological categories are not the only way – and perhaps not even the best way – of grouping Christian churches (p. 48). In fact, that is already the case even in the West. Think of the differences between different cultural communities within the Lutheran World Federation, to say nothing of those within the Orthodox community. Perhaps we can learn that the separation of the "natural" from the "supernatural" is not a particularly biblical way of doing theology (p. 49-50) – all the more since *hyperphysikos* (supernatural) is not a biblical category (try to translate "supernatural" into Hebrew). For the AICs all of nature – that which we believe to understand and that which we believe not to understand – is God's creation and therefore open to unexpected and not yet understood phenomena. A deeper discussion with the leading physicists and scientists could have taught us this long ago.

I am well aware that an intense dialogue with AICs is not easy. In fact, it is a challenge to ecumenists worldwide; and it is a good sign that the WCC is taking the lead in this debate. But we hear some people whispering in our ears: can you really get together with these syncretists?

To this I would like to reply with Leonardo Boff: "Christianity is a syncretism par excellence."[4] If we look at our own churches – and at the Bible – we discover that syncretism belongs essentially to the Christian message.[5] Paul for example wrote his famous hymn on love (1 Cor. 13) by quoting copiously from popular religious sources, as one can learn by consulting any critical commentary. He even manages to talk about love without mentioning Christ. Indeed, if 1 Corinthians 13 were not in the New Testament it would not be recognized as a Christian text. It becomes Christian through the context in which it appears. Or think of our funeral practices. Christ said: "Let the dead bury their dead." Every single funeral he is recorded as having attended was spoiled by his raising the corpse. No theologian would conclude from this that we have to resuscitate the dead instead of burying them decently. We live in a different time and no longer expect the rapture round the corner. So we have had to borrow funeral rites from our Germanic and Celtic ancestors and Christianize them. The same we did with such Christian feasts as Christmas: December 25 is not in the New Testament, but it was an important *holy* day of our forefathers. Even the Bible discloses examples of syncretism. Think of the Magi who according to Matthew found the way to the cradle of Jesus on the basis of pagan astrology while the Bible-reading scribes in Jerusalem got themselves mixed up in a plot to kill the child. Or think of the alliance Christianity has forged with capitalism. It is extremely difficult to discover reflections of the New Testament directives on property and income in our present neo-liberal economic system, in which the churches play an important role. After all Adam Smith, the first theoretician of capitalism, was a Christian theologian.

All this does not suggest that syncretism is by definition an acceptable thing. But it does suggest that before we criticize the AICs because of their syncretism we examine our own praxis and then ask ourselves and each other: under which conditions and when is syncretism not only acceptable but necessary?

So I congratulate the authors of this short book not only because of the valuable research behind it and the information it contains, but also because it throws us back to the biblical message which we must study again. The process of interpretation of the Bible in an ecumenical and cross-cultural way has only begun.

WALTER J. HOLLENWEGER

NOTES

[1] On this see W.J. Hollenweger, "Common Witness Between Catholics and Pentecostals", *Pneuma: Journal of the Society for Pentecostal Studies*, Vol. 18, no.2, 1996, pp.185-216.

[2] Cf. James Dunn, *Unity and Diversity in the New Testament: An Inquiry into the Character of Earliest Christianity*, London, SCM, 1977.

[3] This is liturgically expressed in my "Disciples Mass", celebrated at Fuller Theological Seminary, Pasadena, California, (1996), and published (in German) as *Die Jüngermesse* (with music), Kindhausen, Switzerland, Metanoia Verlag, 1998.

[4] Leonardo Boff, *Church, Charism and Power: Liberation Theology and the Institutional Church*, London, SCM, 1985, pp.92ff.

[5] Detailed in the chapter, "A Plea for a Theologically Responsible Syncretism", in W.J. Hollenweger, *Pentecostalism: Origins and Developments Worldwide*, Peabody, Mass., Hendrickson, 1998.

1. Introduction

In early February 1992 the consecration of the second bishop of the diocese of Cape Coast, Church of the Province of West Africa (Anglican), took place at the Cathedral Church of Christ the King in Cape Coast, Ghana. It was every bit a classical high church Anglican service – the 1662 Book of Common Prayer, *Hymns Ancient and Modern*, colours, incense and all. The bishops of the whole province donned their inherited sartorial gear and were present in splendour and majesty. There could not be a better display of tradition, pomp and circumstance originally minted in England than was displayed in Ghana in 1992.

In the middle of the service a special collection was taken. The music which accompanied it consisted of newer African compositions, originally emanating from the African Independent Churches (AICs). There was much enthusiastic communal singing and dancing. The idiom of the music was very much African, it gripped and grabbed the congregation each and all and none looked excluded. Joy was evident and palpable and, if we may add an interpretative word, there was every sign of the Spirit moving people. The atmosphere was electric, much different from what it had been as the worshippers were going through the inherited English liturgy. That atmosphere – the experience and spirit of gaiety, emotional expression and enthusiasm – was an African response to what has elsewhere been called the North Atlantic captivity of the church in Africa,[1] especially the so-called missionary churches of Northern and Western provenance.

The atmosphere accorded well with African style – spontaneous dancing, singing and enthusiasm at public meetings. What is interesting is that an historic church like the Anglican Church was called and was able, even at the English-minted consecration of a bishop of the "one, holy, catholic and apostolic church", to borrow from the music and style of the African Independent Churches. This is striking because the relationship between so-called historic churches and AICs has been shrouded in polemics. The change in the mood need not be read as a condemnation of the Anglican (English) heritage. But it is "an indication that some African

Christians were dissatisfied with the imported church structures, patterns of ministry, liturgical forms, hymnody and architectural buildings which had been introduced into Africa by Western Christian missionaries".[2]

The polemics have arisen for all sorts of reasons, not least that some AICs broke away from the mission churches. The Church of the Lord (Aladura), which is a member church of the WCC, broke away from the Church Missionary Society (Anglican) in Nigeria.[3] The Musama Disco Christo Church of the Gold Coast (Ghana) broke away from the Methodist Church of the Gold Coast.[4] In Southern Rhodesia, now Zimbabwe, Johane Maranke and the nucleus of the leadership of the African Apostolic Church of Johane Maranke (AACJM), known among the Shona as *vaPostori* (Apostles), broke away from the American Methodist Mission.

The language of "breaking away" needs to be nuanced. Some AICs broke away from historic churches out of administrative or doctrinal differences. On the other hand, the Church of the Lord (Aladura) came into being as a result of a Pentecostal resurgence which the Church Missionary Society (Anglican) felt unable to countenance and for that reason expelled the men and women who eventually founded their own brand of AIC. Christ Apostolic Church of Nigeria was formed by a group who broke away from the Anglican Church as a result of doctrinal influence from a North American religious group. Thus it is not always the case that AICs chose to break away; sometimes they were pushed out by the historic churches which could not hear and feel the yearnings of Africans as they searched after God.

Without going further into the reasons for the schism and the acrimony, we may remark that the historic churches have often applied *etic* interpretations to the AICs. "Etic" is the term scholars use for interpretations by which observers and researchers read meanings into a phenomenon, in the process imposing their biases and interpretations. This realization has led Pobee to write that "the historic churches at best have been suspicious of AICs, regarding them as a heathenization of Christianity. Not surprisingly the AICs have rarely found a place in the ecumenical movement."[5] In consequence, these two streams of the "one, holy, catholic and apostolic church" have often looked at each other with anything but Christian charity.

However, with the passing of time we must endeavour to see each other in a new light and not perpetuate the language of polemics. So we would plead for an *emic* approach – one which reads the story of AICs through the eyes of the actors and participants in the particular tradition. Indeed, the very fact that the Anglican diocese of Cape Coast was able to draw on music from the AIC tradition is a reminder that it is possible and necessary to transcend the culture of polemics which has prevailed in our relations.

Anyone who dares to write about another denomination or religion must bear in mind the simple truth that it is a believer and participant of a tradition who is best able to understand and articulate that tradition. Moreover, there are epistemological factors – that is, issues of understanding and interpreting what is observed – entailed in any attempt to make abstractions regarding the meaning of a belief system, especially one to which the interpreter does not subscribe.[6] In this book we have consciously attempted a sympathetic reading of the story of AICs.

The acronym AIC may stand for a number of things: African Independent Churches, African Initiatives in Christianity, African Instituted Churches, African Indigenous Churches. Some would call them African Christian Initiatives. The acronym specifies a category of church in Africa to be distinguished from "mission" or "historic" or "mainline" or "established" churches. Turner defines an African Independent Church as "a church which has been founded in Africa, by Africans and primarily for Africans".[7] The note of African origin indicates that a primary characteristic of this genre is commitment to the adaptation of the gospel to African needs, life-view and life-style. Further, the designation hints that AICs are a protest movement, protesting against the North Atlantic and Western captivity of the gospel as represented by the historic churches.

Turner's definition helps to distinguish between AICs and the gropings of historic churches for the Africanization of mission churches. Initially the historic churches sought, on the basis of their European model, the Christianization of the African, but the model remained basically a European arte-fact. AICs on the other hand seek the Africanization of Chris-tianity in outlook, form and scope, distinct from and without administrative connections with foreign mission-based orga-nizations.

Protest movements they may be, but AICs also claim to be Christian and church, and thus to belong to the "one holy, catholic and apostolic church" and the one household of God. They may be quite different from the mission-founded or historic churches. But as part of the one household of God they have ecumenical significance.

Despite the merits of Turner's clear definition of an African Independent Church, we would prefer the term "African Initiatives in Christianity". While it is true that in earlier times the mission churches were colonial churches, today they are nearly all independent, even if they retain aspects of their origins. So it is incorrect to apply "indepen-dent" exclusively to AICs; it is true also of the historic churches. What is unique about AICs is their character as *African* initiatives and, therefore, in accordance with the African genius and culture and ethos.

The World Council of Churches today has among its membership in Africa four churches from the AIC tradition: the African Church of the Holy Spirit (Kakanega, Kenya); the African Israel Nineveh Church, (Kisumu, Kenya), founded by Paul David Zakayo Kivuli (1896-1974); the Church of the Lord (Aladura) (Shagamu, Nigeria); Eglise de Jésus Christ sur la Terre par son envoyé spécial Simon Kim-bangu (EJCSK), more commonly known as Kimbanguist Church (Lutendele, Zaïre). Their very presence in the WCC points to an enlargement of the ecumenical arena. If in 1948 when the WCC came into being, it was largely Protestant with some Orthodox, today AICs are also at the table, taking part in the discussion. On the face of it they may look like strangers to one another. But there is growing consciousness that AICs belong with Protestants, Orthodox and Roman Catholics to the one household of God. Mission-founded churches and AICs may differ from one another in ethos, style, theological emphases, worship and spirituality; but they are siblings in God's family. Dare we disenfranchise or unchurch the other?

In 1967 David Barrett, on the basis of research in 34 African countries, estimated that there were 6.9 million AIC adherents in 5031 separate movements in Africa.[8] They were distributed further as follows: Central Africa 1.2 million, East Africa about 1 million, North Africa 12,000, Southern Africa 3.2 million and West Africa about 1 million. In 1993 Patrick Johnstone put the total figure at some 39 million, with about 20,000 Pentecostal "Charismatics" in sub-Saharan Africa.[9]

With all the reservations one may have about the precision of these statistics, they do suggest that AICs have grown phenomenally in overall membership and that they represent a central development of Christianity in the Africa of the 20th century. This indicates that the landscape of world Christianity is changing. There is no way we can talk of world Christianity, much less Christianity in Africa, without taking account of this genre of AICs.

Barrett noted that in 1967 the 1 million AIC adherents in Zaïre were in 500 groups. The 600,000 adherents in Nigeria were in 500 groups, the 600,000 in Kenya in 160 groups. In Ghana 200,000 AIC adherents were in 200 groups. Half a million adherents in Zimbabwe were in 100 groups. South Africa alone probably has over 4000 groups. Again, no matter what we make of these figures, they do point not only to the diversity in the genre of AICs but also to their divisive (or, as the scholars put it, fissiparous) nature. As such they present a particular challenge to the ecumenical vocation of the people of God.

In this context the language of "one holy, catholic and apostolic church" may raise some eyebrows. These "marks of the church" are proclaimed by the Nicene Creed. But it is important to remember that each of these marks has come up for challenge or rethinking at some point in the history of the church. For example, the Great Schism between the churches of the East and the West in 1054 tested the oneness of the church. And, indeed, in post-second world war ecumenism, the oneness of the church is the issue at stake. The mark of holiness was the critical issue in the Donatist controversy of the fourth century, at a time when the church was making the transition from a church of the martyrs to a church of the majority. In the Reformation of the 16th century, apostolicity was the issue at stake. In today's world, characterized as the global village, it is perhaps the mark of catholicity which takes on a new significance for the church of Jesus Christ. The AICs focus in a particular and special way the issue of how the church may maintain the necessary balance between the global and the local. Robert Schreiter has written:

> Catholicity has traditionally been understood as [the church's] extension through the world and its fullness of the truth handed down from the apostles. Now communication – including issues of culture, identity and social change – becomes a third and necessary addition to the theological concept of catholicity. It is perhaps only by such an addition that some of the struggles so apparent in theology today – about concepts of the church, appropriate forms of inculturation, commitment to liberation and possible reconciliation – can be addressed effectively. This theological addendum gives the new catholicity concreteness.[10]

This chapter has assumed a distinction between two types of African churches: AICs and those called variously "main-line", "historic", "established" or "mission" churches. But whatever the terminology, churches in both categories claim first to be Christian and second to belong to the one church of Jesus Christ. The very existence of these two distinct groups in Africa reminds us of the diversity and divergence within the "one holy, catholic and apostolic church" as a whole. In this connection we should perhaps also recall how the imperial model of the Roman Empire helped to shape the language of "one, holy, catholic and apostolic". Might the emergence and growth of the AICs require us to revisit this terminology?

How helpful is the imperial model as we survey the multi-plicity of expressions of the body of Christ in these new and more pluralist times? To this we shall return later.

While Anglican, Orthodox and Roman Catholic tradi-tions, with their commitment to the ecumenical councils of the early centuries, emphasize the unity, holiness, catholicity and apostolicity of the church, many others in the Protestant tradition would place the accent on three criteria of the true church: "incorruptible proclamation of the Word", the right use of the sacraments of baptism and eucharist, and the exer-cise of discipline. The category of AIC urges us to desist from indiscriminately applying our own respective *notae ecclesiae* to others (here we are reminded of the distinction between *emic* and *etic* approaches mentioned above), but also to search for further criteria for measuring AICs. Such criteria might include such considerations as the role of the church in society, incarnational theology, perceptions of sal-vation. This, we suggest, must be on the agenda of the ecu-menical movement and of the WCC.

We may conclude this introductory chapter by returning to the frequent description of AICs as protest movements – protests against the style and theology of the so-called his-toric churches. We noted above that this description needs nuancing. But it is also inadequate if it draws attention away from the creativity and originality which AICs exhibit:

> Their creative response to God's Word is co-determined by far more than just an apparently negative reaction to mission. Their interpretations of the Bible, distinctive forms of worship and modified rites are part of an authentic, indigenous response to the gospel, an independent momentum free of European super-vision and of the radical spirit which would have characterized a real reaction to mission...
>
> The Independent Churches' real attraction for members and growth derives from their original, creative attempts to relate the good news of the gospel in a meaningful and symbolically intelligible way to the innermost needs of Africa. In doing so they are in a process of – and have to a large extent already suc-ceeded – in creating truly African *havens of belonging*.[11]

8

NOTES

1 John S. Pobee, "African Instituted Churches", in N. Lossky et al., eds, *Dictionary of the Ecumenical Movement*, Geneva, WCC, 1991, pp.10-12.

2 Edward W. Fashole-Luke, "The Quest for an African Christian Theology", in *Mission as Liberation: Third World Theologies*, Pretoria, Unisa, 1989, p.1.

3 Cf. H. Turner, *Church of the Lord, Aladura*, Oxford, Clarendon, 1967.

4 Cf. C.G. Baëta, *Prophetism in Ghana*, London, SCM Press, 1962, pp.39ff.

5 John S. Pobee, *loc. cit.*, p.11.

6 R.A. Hahn, "Understanding Belief", *Current Anthropology*, Vol. 14, no. 3, 1973, pp.207-29.

7 H.W. Turner, "A Typology of African Religious Movements", *Journal of Religion in Africa*, Vol. 1, no. 1, 1967, p.17.

8 David B. Barrett, *Schism and Renewal in Africa: An Analysis of Six Thousand Contemporary Religious Movements*, London, Oxford U.P., 1968, p.98, Table II.

9 Patrick Johnstone, *Operation World*, Carlisle, UK, OM Publishing, 1993.

10 Robert J. Schreiter, *The New Catholicity: Theology between the Global and the Local*, Maryknoll, NY, Orbis, 1997, p.xi.

11 M.L. Daneel, *Quest for Belonging*, Gweru, Zimbabwe, Mambo Press, 1987, pp.22, 25, 100f.

2. In the Beginning

Sociologists and anthropologists have demonstrated that *homo africanus homo religiosus radicaliter* – the African is a radically religious person, religious at the core of his or her being.[1] Africans' communal activities and their social institutions are inextricably bound up with religion and the spirit world. This is not to say that Africans are sacralists; rather, Africans seem unable to explain life and its mysteries without some reference to the supernatural.

Christians, especially missionaries of a certain type, have tended to talk as if Christianity is the best thing that happened to Africans. While we have no doubt that Christianity has a creditable record in Africa, particularly through the contributions missionaries and churches made through the social services, Africans also have other opinions on this. Thus, for example, an Asante prince once said to the Rev. T.R. Picot, a Methodist missionary:

> The Bible is not a book for us. God at the beginning gave the Bible to the white people, another to the Cramos [Muslims] and fetish to us... We know God already ourselves. We will never embrace your religion, for it would make our people proud. It is your religion which has ruined the Fanti country, weakened their power and brought down the high man on a level with the low man.[2]

This African royalist was not only rejecting the attitudes of superiority of Europe to Africa, the Caucasian to the Negroid, the Christian to the non-Christian, but also pointing to some very negative aspects of the incoming Christian religion, namely that Christianity is a religion which induces pride and attitudes of superiority and thus is destructive of social structures. In any case, Africans had their own religion before the advent of Christianity. The missionary church has itself to blame for this criticism of its work because, while we may concede that mission is about the transformation of people and society, it is also true that the missionary practice of *tabula rasa* – wiping the slate clean – made Christianity foreign and missionaries the bearers of an alien culture to Africa. The rise of AICs may be seen in part as a protest by Africans against this missionary practice of *tabula rasa* (without denying the insights of Daneel cited above regarding AICS as much more than a protest).

Let us take another African response, this one from a chief from Akropong, Akwapim, Eastern Region of Ghana, who said to a missionary of the Basel Mission (Protestant) named Andreas Riis: "When God created the world, he made books for the white man and fetishes for the black man. But if you can show us some black man who can read the white man's books, then we shall surely follow you."[3] This points to the fact that there were different motives for Africans embracing Christianity. Initially the social services provided by the missions (education and health) attracted people to come to or be near the church. More recently, we may recall that the support the world church gave to those who were struggling against racism in Zimbabwe and South Africa or, more generally, the humanitarian assistance from Christians, churches and ecumenical bodies to Africans in need has attracted people to the Christian faith in Africa. Such activity sometimes encourages Africans to see the World Council of Churches as yet another non-governmental organization or aid agency. But it would be a mistake to focus only on the social, political and economic contributions. There is also a deeply religious and spiritual quest. This quest helps us to understand how persons nurtured in the womb of the historic churches may at some point go over to an AIC. Rather than get into polemics, it is better to ask: what is it that the historic churches have not done right, which encourages some of their members to "vote with their feet" and join other churches?

K.A. Busia, a sociologist from Ghana and a staunch Methodist lay preacher, wrote more than 30 years ago that "those who have been responsible for the propagation of the Christian gospel in other lands and cultures have not shown sufficient awareness of the need for an encounter between the Christian religion and the cosmology of the peoples outside European culture and traditions. It is this which has made Christianity either alien or superficial or both."[4]

When some people – not only in Europe and America but also in Africa – hear such language, they immediately begin to worry about attempts to "heathenize" the Christian faith, forgetting that the expressions of the Christian faith which the missionaries transplanted to Africa bore heavy marks of earlier European cultures which would equally merit the name "heathen". And every age and every church must go through a similar creative exercise if the Christian faith is to come alive for new contexts. Busia describes the task thus:

> The concept of "African" Christianity does not mean that there is a version of Christianity that is African, any more than that there is European Christianity. Christ as the Truth and the Way belongs to all ages and all climes. There are universal and eternal elements of Christianity that cannot be nationalized or regionalized: yet Christianity enjoins a way of life to be lived in society, and this must find expression in human relations and institutions. It is in that context that cultural patterns are relevant. It is this expression of Christianity in an African milieu that we are all seeking. The search affords opportunities for cooperation and interchange between clergy and layman, between different denominations of the church.[5]

Thus the emergence of the AICs is a call for all cultures to be present in the ecumenical discussion, which should not focus only on doctrinal issues. It is a reminder that God's world and God's church are much bigger and broader than our own respective little turfs. God's *oikos*, household, includes more than "our kind" and our friends. Thus we must develop cultures that are welcoming and inclusive. Revelation 7:9-10 gives a very eloquent image of the ecumenical vocation: "I looked, and there was a great multitude that no one could count, from *every nation*, from *all tribes* and *peoples* and *languages*, standing up before the throne and before the Lamb, robed in white, with palm branches in their hands. They cried out in a loud voice, saying 'Salvation belongs to our God who is seated on the throne, and to the Lamb'." The African must also be there in God's household, alongside all the people from every nation. This ultimate ecumenical vision is to be realized in worship together before the Lamb, and none of our distinctions of race or language is crucial.

Notwithstanding what we have said about the growth of Christianity, we must not forget that Africa presents us with religious pluralism. In most of our nations we have in addition to our several Christian denominations other religions, principally African Traditional Religions and Islam. Christian churches do not always enjoy majority positions. In places like the Gambia and Senegal, Christians are in a clear minority in a sea of Muslims. But although the dynamics of our lives together in our respective nations are different, we need to work together to live in peace, in which we can find the security and quiet to worship the one God and Creator of all and as Christians to witness credibly to those who do not belong to the church. The statement of the African royalist quoted earlier in this chapter reminds us of the need always to be mindful of living our missionary vocation and the ecumenical imperative with a sense of the plurality of the world.

In the beginning God created the earth, including humanity. Perhaps the testimony of Paul about the Gentiles has a lesson for us: "What can be known about God is plain to them [the Gentiles] because God has shown it to them. Ever since the creation of the world [God's] eternal power and divine nature, invisible though they are, have been understood and seen through the things God has made" (Rom. 1:19-20). The application is obvious: in God's plans God has communicated something to the Africans, which must be built upon. The AICs seek to bring an African sense of God's eternal power and divine nature to an understanding of the triune God. And so, to quote Daneel again,

> their churches expand because of the unique development of a missionary vision, and... they are able to act without being biased in any way by denominational differences and prejudices. Their adapted rites with regard to faith-healing, rainmaking, fertility, magic and the like are not necessarily or exclusively prompted by pragmatic considerations covering the proselytizing value of such adaptation, but also products of a conscious, existential involvement with the "good news" of the

Christian God, regardless of the prescriptions or views of some Western-oriented mission church.[6]

To this we may add a longstanding judgment by the late and eminent missiologist Max Warren: "It is a cardinal assumption of the Christian mission that whatever the changes in the world the gospel, God's good news for man, remains unchanged. Nevertheless it calls for new interpretations as man's vocabulary of experience widens and deepens. To this exciting task of interpretation the Christian mission is, I believe, of necessity being called."[7] AICs represent this vocation of Christian mission to couch the good news of God for humanity in their particular language and contexts.

NOTES

[1] K.A. Busia, *Africa in Search of Democracy*, London, Routledge & Kegan Paul, 1967; Busia, *The Position of the Chief in the Modern Political System of Ashante*, London, Frank Cass, 1968.
[2] Cited in G.G. Findlay and W.W. Holdsworth, *The History of the Wesleyan Methodist Society*, London, Epworth, 1922, Vol. 4, p.173.
[3] *A Hundred Years: The Story of the Presbyterian Training College, Akropong*, Akropong, Gold Coast, Presbyterian Press, 1948, p.16.
[4] K.A. Busia, "Has the Christian Faith Been Adequately Represented?", *International Review of Mission*, Vol. 50, 1963, pp.86-89; see also his contribution "The Commitment of the Laity in the Growth of the Church and the Integral Development of Africa", *Laity Today*, special number, 1972, pp.239-46.
[5] Busia, "The Commitment of the Laity", *loc. cit.*, p.241.
[6] Daneel, *Quest for Belonging*, p.101.
[7] M.A.C. Warren, "Political Realities and the Christian Mission", in J.S. Pobee, ed., *Religion in a Pluralistic Society*, Leiden, E.J. Brill, 1976, pp.119-20.

3. Christ Arrives in Africa

It is a common assumption, particularly among Protestants, that Christianity was a relative latecomer to Africa. As a matter of fact, Christianity came to Upper Egypt and Sudan between Aswan and Khartoum in the first century (cf. Acts 8:26-40). That church moulded the fortunes of Christianity for nearly a thousand years through its monks, its martyrs and its renowned catechetical school of higher learning at Alexandria, presided over by Clement of Alexandria (c. 150-215). The lively and constructive theological activity there is exemplified by the presence of the Gnostics, who propagated esoteric teachings in the second century, and the Arians, whose teaching was to be declared heretical.

The story of Alexandrian theology is the story of attempts to interpret Christian teachings in Greek philosophical terms. Perhaps every attempt to translate the gospel across cultures and languages carries with it some danger of overstating the case and of others seeing this as deviation from standard teaching and eventually declaring it heresy.

A collection of the New Testament writings was circulating in Egypt by the early second century, and translations of the Scriptures into Coptic, the national Egyptian language, were made in the third century. We are also reminded by this story of what was perhaps the first systematic mission – to natives outside Alexandria. But the point we would underscore here is that there was never a monochrome Christianity. The notion of "one holy, catholic and apostolic church" is never to be understood as implying uniformity of style and practice. Already then the vernacular paradigm was in vogue and characteristic of mission. Within the one church there was a Greek church and a Latin church and a Coptic church and so on.

One of the children of Egypt was Origen (c. 185-253). Not only did he succeed the great theologian Clement of Alexandria as the leader of the catechetical school but while staying in Caesarea he also converted St Gregory of Cappadocia in Asia Minor. Origen's work laid the foundations for scholarly analysis of Scripture and developed a coherent theology of the nature of God, revelation and salvation. By these efforts he sought to forge links extending the chain of apostolic teaching and example. Here we highlight him in order to emphasize the importance of interpreting Christian teachings in the contemporary context in a manner that shows links with apostolic teaching.

Several centuries later, heavy taxation, social and religious restrictions in Egypt and the stern repression of Cyrus, patriarch and representative of the emperor Heraclitus (610-614), caused many Copts to feel increasing disaffection towards the Orthodox communion and consequently to welcome as deliverers the Arabs who arrived in 640 under Amir ibn al As. And so, today, amidst the Muslim majority in Egypt, stands the Coptic Church of Egypt, which is closer to the faith of the Orthodox church but remains an isolated national church.

Within the organization of the WCC, Egypt, which belongs to both the Middle East Council of Churches and the All Africa Conference of Churches, is treated as part of the former region; and we shall not devote further attention to Egypt in this short book. But we recognize Egypt and its ecclesial legacy as part of what the continent of Africa has contributed to the *oikoumene*.

On the other side of North Africa was the Maghreb – Proconsular Africa in Roman times, Morocco, Tunisia and Algeria today. The recorded history of Christianity here goes back as far as 180, when a martyrdom of Christians was recorded at Scilli, near Carthage. The very fact of persecution suggests that the church was significant enough to attract the attention of the Roman authorities of Proconsular Africa. The thriving church there at that early date produced some of the intellectual giants of the Christian story, among them Cyprian of Carthage (d. c. 258) and Augustine of Hippo (354-430), as well as innumerable village churches.

Although this church was not in filial relationship with the Church of Rome and had considerable Eastern church influence on it, it became the first centre of Latin theology. Tertullian (c. 155-225) represented the exact and legal spirit of the Latins, establishing the theological terminology of the

West in respect of the Trinity, immortalizing such terms as *substance* and *person* in speaking of God. The very Latin flavour of sacramental doctrine in this church was established largely by Augustine of Hippo (354-430). Cyprian of Carthage also left important legacies with regard to the teaching about the church. Christianity in Proconsular Africa was very biblical. The accounts of the Scillitan Martyrs and Tertullian's *Prescription Against the Heretics* denied heretics the use of the Scriptures. This church also produced the *Itala*, the earliest Latin translation of the Greek Bible.

The rigorism of the church of Proconsular Africa produced several schisms in the church, notably around the teachings of Montanism, an apocalyptic movement in the latter part of the second century which recruited Tertullian of Carthage, and Donatism. It is worth taking a closer look at each of these in connection with our purposes here.

Montanism took its name from its founder Montanus, who had been a pagan priest in Phrygia until his conversion in 155:

> He began prophesying, declaring that he had been possessed by the Holy Spirit. Soon two women, Priscilla and Maximilla, also began prophesying. This in itself was not new, for at that time, at least in some churches, women were allowed to prophesy. What was new, and gave rise to serious misgivings, was that Montanus and his followers claimed that their movement was the beginning of a new age. Just as in Jesus Christ a new age had begun, so was a still newer age beginning in the outpouring of the Spirit. This new age was characterized by a more rigorous moral life, just as the Sermon on the Mount was itself more demanding than the law of the Old Testament.[1]

The details of the story of Montanus are echoed in varying ways and degrees in the stories of AICs. Montanism, originating in Phrygia, came from a land and culture which set much store by spirit mediums. This tradition also made room for vehicles of revelation other than the Scriptures. Both of these elements are not uncommon in AICs. At issue here are the experience of the Holy Spirit, the role of prophecy and moral rigour – partly because of a quite literal-

ist interpretation of Scripture, partly out of opposition to the
intense secularization of Christianity.

The importance we attach to the story of Montanism
leads us to cite an extended passage which points to some of
the key issues at stake when we think of AICs. Peter L'Huillier writes:

> Montanism had grown up in Phrygia between 156 and 172 as a
> prophetic and charismatic movement ending up in illuminism.
> It built itself into an exclusive sect. The Montanists believed in
> millenarianism, and they exalted abstinence from sexual activ-
> ity to an exaggerated degree. To what degree did they diverge
> from Orthodox trinitarian doctrine? On this point, the opinions
> of the fathers do not agree: St Epiphanius categorically affirmed
> that "concerning the Father, the Son and the Holy Spirit they
> have the same feelings as the holy catholic church". St Jerome,
> on the other hand, accused them of Sabellianism. As for St
> Basil, he mentioned "that they were obviously heretics because
> they blasphemed against the Holy Spirit by attributing the name
> of the Paraclete in an improper and shameful way to Montanus
> and Priscilla". For the bishop of Caesarea, the nullity of their
> baptism was beyond question. This was also the opinion of the
> fathers of Laodicea. The reason for rejecting the baptism of the
> Sabellians was obvious: they did not admit the real distinction
> between the divine persons; they could not, therefore, really
> baptize in the name of the Father, the Son and the Holy Spirit.[2]

We quote this to indicate how, as in the early church,
there are today almost bound to be diverse and divergent esti-
mates of the AICs. The contemporary evaluation of AICs can
learn from how the churches evaluated the Montanists. The
key issues remain how they measure up to the Christian doctrine of the Trinity, how their portraiture of the Holy Spirit is
acceptable as a Christian statement and how the common rite
of baptism measures up to the thinking and tradition of the
one holy, catholic and apostolic church. These are the three
issues around which ecumenical dialogue should be held. We
would plead that it is not helpful to proceed in a judgmental
manner, using the language of "heresy". The question for
ecumenical dialogue, bilateral or multilateral, between the
AICs and the WCC is twofold: do the member churches of

18

the WCC find themselves in the self-description of AICs with regard to the three questions set out above? And do the AICs find themselves in the self-understanding of the churches in the WCC on these three issues?

Part of the issue in evaluating AICs is the place of prophecy and prophetic movements in the institutional church with all its established (if not ossified) institutions. Do those who subscribe to the model of church as institution have the right to judge on the basis of their own criteria those in a prophetic movement? How may the model of church as institution co-exist with church as movement in the one body of Christ?

Let us also return to the point about moral rigour. Their detractors often consider AICs as morally lax, frequently pointing to how some allow polygamy. But this attitude is rather myopic. Those who leave the historic churches to join AICs do so because of a high and exalted quest: they are looking for an experience of the Spirit as power, which they do not seem to find in the historic churches. Accompanying that search are very rigorist attitudes.

Donatism for its part also reflected the social and material antagonisms of the church. North Africa was the home of three groups: Romans who were Christians, Punics who were much Romanized and therefore fairly Christianized, Berbers who were natives and seemingly Christianized. The strength of the Donatists was among the Berber Numidians, and Donatism thus represented a nationalistic revolt against the Latinization of the church and society. The simple labelling of Donatists as heretics obscures the very important fact that in 336 Donatism had the support of 270 bishops and by the end of the fourth century 400 bishops – this in spite of the close alliance between the Catholic Church and the Roman power in Africa. Such was the Berbers' hatred of Latin Christianity that they supported Hassan, who took Carthage in 697, and subsequently joined the Arabs to conquer Spain in 711, setting the seal on their conversion to Islam. Like Montanism, the Donatist schism also raised theological issues: the nature of the church and the validity of the sacraments.

But the church of North Africa capitulated before the Muslim onslaught in the sixth and seventh centuries. Roman rule in North Africa had begun in 146 BC with the sack of Carthage and was nailed down with the conquest of Mauretania in AD 40. Here we need not go into the details of the long process of Romanization of North Africa, except to repeat that the Maghreb had three nations: Roman, Punic and Berber. Part of the reason for the capitulation of the church before the Muslims was that the church and the Christian faith were of the Roman oppressor and never really engaged the native Berber. When the Arab invaders came, Elizabeth Isichei writes, they

> encountered a Christian culture largely confined to the towns and weakened both by sectarian divisions and by the invasions of, first, Aryan Vandals, and then of Berber nomads, Lawata, "ignorant of the Christian God". Gradually the Berbers of the North-West became, first, *mawali*, then Muslims. There were also economic inducements to conversion: the chance of joining the armies that conquered Spain, and freedom from poll tax.[3]

This story of Christianity in the Maghreb has two important lessons for our subject. First, the church of Roman North Africa never really engaged the native Berber. It remained an intruder. Its structure and being were foreign, and it was not asking nor answering the questions the native Berbers were asking. For a religion whose central affirmation is that "the Word became flesh *and lived among us*" (John 1:14), this failure represents an appalling insensitivity. The AICs of today are posing that ancient concern in a new way.

A second lesson we may draw from the early history of the Christian Church in North Africa is that divisions in the church are ultimately not in the best interests of the church itself. The divisive element of "nationalism" apparent in the rise of Donatism is also identifiable in some of the AICs of our day, especially in their commitment to worshipping God as Africans. Such divisions not only undermine the credibility of the church when it makes certain claims about itself, particularly the claim that it is called to be God's instrument for the reconciliation of the world, but also sap its energies.

We have devoted some time to this period of church history to make three general points: that Christianity in Africa goes back fairly early; that North African Christianity of the early centuries had a significant impact on the theology of the world Christianity; and that it manifested schisms and disunity fairly early on, some elements of which are not unlike what the AICs signify and represent. The church of North Africa failed because of its identification with the unpopular imperial government and its lack of unity, adaptive capacity and missionary dynamism.

Africa south of the Sahara met Christianity during the 450-year period of conquest and colonial rule which has been called the Vasco da Gama era (1492-1947). This was initially linked with Portuguese ascendancy. By the Treaty of Tordesillias (1494), Pope Alexander VI made the Portuguese king responsible for founding and supporting missionaries and endowing bishoprics in Africa and part of Brazil. This chapter of African history was a mixture of adventure, study, politics, trade, crusading and evangelism. The crusader spirit was directed against both the Muslims and the African culture. Two of its manifestations were the ideology of *requerimiento*, according to which natives were obliged to obey the Christian ideals of the king of Portugal or face hostilities, and the missionary practice of *tabula rasa*, which we have mentioned earlier. Both of these reflected Western Christian ethnocentrism, which relegated non-Europeans to the category of degenerate savages who had lost the original purity of religion which was Adam's.

If this phase was at the outset very much a Roman Catholic affair, the Protestants did come, particularly in the late 18th century. Despite their deep differences with the Catholics on issues of doctrine and practice, the Protestants operated with some of the same ideologies which had driven the Roman Catholic mission in Africa: a Eurocentric worldview, a crusading spirit and mentality, and a confusion of evangelism and politics, deepened by the dawning of the age of colonialism.

A landmark of African church history to which we should call attention here is the 19th-century development called Ethiopianism, which flourished first in West Africa, then in Southern Africa. The impulse for this movement is at least twofold. One was the missionary-oriented "Africa for the Africans" movement, a typical example of which was the African Methodist Episcopal Church. The other was the "three-self" principle associated with Rufus Anderson, foreign secretary of the American Board for Foreign Missions (1832-1866), and Henry Venn, a secretary of the Church Missionary Society (1841-1872). This principle was committed to the development of self-governing, self-propagating and self-supporting churches, so that foreign mission would before long give way to the development of indigenous and independent mission.

Ethiopianism represented an African remonstration against the European captivity of the gospel. Its sources and motives were complex, as G. Shepperson observes:

> the stimulus of European ecclesial secession; reaction against over-strict disciplining of African converts by European missionaries; the desire of some African separatist ministers to increase their personal power and status by administering church property and monies; the creation of tribal churches in which due respect was paid to African customs; and a rejection of the colour bar in many European-controlled churches.[4]

An important feature of Ethiopianism is that it was most evident in areas where there were concentrations of highly educated Africans who felt marginalized in both church and nation. Some of the great names of this movement were Edward Wilmot Blyden (1832-1912), James Africanus Beale Horton (1835-1883), Rev. (later Bishop) James Johnson, Rev. Esien Ukpabio and David Brown Vincent (1860-1917), who changed his name to Mojola Agbebi and his wife's to Adeotan. This name change may seem trivial or facile unless we recognize that the so-called Christian names which African converts were obliged to take at baptism, giving up their African names, were not always exactly biblical names but names coming from European history such as George or

William. For Africans names are more than labels of identification. Names are closely linked to one's identity: there is
something important in a name. This whole issue points
again to a yearning for an African incarnation or tabernacling
of the Word, an African church in which Africans are present
as Africans and not in the image and likeness of Europeans,
and a vision of Africans around the throne of God with all
others, each with their own respective identities.[5]

Against this background, Ethiopianism might be
described as proto-nationalism. This can be illustrated from
the history of the church in West Africa, where missionaries
of the 19th and early 20th centuries were imbued with a certain paternalism – or as some would call it, racism – in spite
of the three-self principle mentioned above. A good example
was the response of Adolphus Mann, the CMS local secretary in Nigeria, to the proposal to make Samuel Adjai
Crowther, a freed slave who became a great figure in the missionary endeavours of the CMS, the first African bishop of
the Niger:

> The native mind wants a guide, a stimulus, a superintendence,
> and this is the very thing you go about to take away from him
> through the *Native Church*. There will be no more the whole-
> some influence of the white man's energy... The absolute inde-
> pendence of the Native I dread... When I am no admirer of the
> Native independence I am so from the best of feelings for the
> African man; that he may be largely profited, for more than
> time allowed, by a wise presidence of the white man.[6]

Ethiopianism represented a movement against such paternalism. Thus an article in the *Lagos Observer* of 1886 carries
this appeal: "A revolution must occur in the Episcopalian
Church... We cry aloud complainingly... and a voice in reply
comes to us ringing the word in our ears: *Secession! Secession! Secession!*"[7] In this sense Ethiopianism may be seen as
embryonic nationalism. But it was far more than politics don-
ning the cloak of religion; much more importantly, it reflected
a yearning for an African church in consonance with the
Africans' own ethos, their natural and "national" characteristics. Thus Coker, the founder of the African Church, records

that he set up his church when the Spirit spoke to him thus: "Coker, I want you to go and preach that polygamists become full members of my church."[8] This was a movement for inculturation in the area of plural marriages and the use of the vernacular. Particularly in colonial times, the AICs created little islands of African identity and autonomy.

Ethiopianism thus represented a blend of several African aspirations. First, it incorporated an appeal to the early African church heritage. Second, it expressed a yearning after an authentic African spirituality, for the spirituality inherited from the missionaries was foreign to Africans. Third, it asserted the validity of African cultural identity in the church: Africans were tired of being cast in the image and likeness of European-American missionaries. Fourth, this search for African cultural identity was also in varying degrees a quest for pan-Africanism. To the extent that the missionary-colonial church was not prepared to meet these African aspirations, the movement had only the option of separatism.

We would underscore that Ethiopianism is not to be confused with the Ethiopian Orthodox Church, which is also an ancient church that represents an amalgam of Judaic and Christian practices, African and European rituals. That church is also a very African church, but it is quite different from the movement which came to bear the name Ethiopianism.[9]

This complex of African concerns lies at the heart of what, particularly during the Independence Era (1947-), has been manifest as AICs. Some of these AICs in fact emerged well before the Independence Era. For example, the Kimbanguist Church came into being in 1921 in what was then the Belgian Congo. Its adherents today are mostly in the Democratic Republic of Congo (formerly Zaïre), Angola, Rwanda, Burundi, Central African Republic, Chad, Zambia and Uganda – all of which became independent much after 1921. Similarly, the Musama Disco Christo Church (MDCC) started around 1922 as a breakaway from the Methodist Church of the Gold Coast, where independence came in 1957.

24

It is against this background that we must see the AICs.
They have different emphases. But they are together seeking
to communicate at the wave-length of Africans through their
worldview, their non-conceptual medium of theologizing
(for example, dance and music), their exorcisms and their
other ways of accommodating traditional African religious
beliefs and practices.

Our survey of this history from the years of the early
church to the 19th century illustrates that African Christianity has been trying all along and in diverse ways to send missionary Christianity a message which it has not heard or
appreciated. That heritage locates AICs and gives them their
significance in world Christianity. Their persistent quest is a
necessary reminder that Caucasian mintings of the "one holy,
catholic and apostolic church" are not and cannot be the
exclusive or the total expression of the fullness of Christ and
his body. We may push this point further to argue that as long
as the ecumenical movement is described only in terms of
dialogue between Orthodox, Protestant and Roman Catholic
churches it is not complete. AICs stand in the world church
to remind us that the ecumenical movement must represent
more than the coming together of the Greek and Latin traditions of Christianity and their descendants in Europe and
North America. The movement should rediscover that the
vernacular paradigm, which characterized the earliest church
from the day of Pentecost and was reflected in the translation
and transmission of the Bible, is of the essence of ecumenism. No group is excluded. AICs are a testimony that
today as at Pentecost (Acts 2:10) Africans are still hearing
the word of God in their own languages.

NOTES

[1] Justo L. González, *The Story of Christianity*, Vol. 1, San Francisco,
Harper & Row, 1984, p.76.
[2] Peter L'Huillier, *The Church of the Ancient Councils*, New York, St
Vladimir's Seminary Press, 1996, p.134.

4. African Initiatives in Christianity

The terminology of "mother"-"daughter" churches tends to obscure that even if Christianity came to Africa south of the Sahara via Europe and North America, the Africans were not just passive recipients. Native catechists and evangelists were the unsung heroes of African church history.[1] These people, whose names are mostly unremembered, were in fact the ones who nurtured the faith of the Africans who would later be baptized by the missionaries. Furthermore, Africans have not only received the artefacts of the North Atlantic but have also reconstructed them. Thus Africans have understood the church according to the paradigm of the traditional extended family, wanting to stress the sense of belonging and of community. This quest of Africans, deeply rooted in their self-understanding of reality and being, has led many to walk out of the so-called historic churches, where they have found no satisfaction in the very individualistic understanding of the Christian faith and church.

Similarly, the priest in the AIC is "not just an officiant or mediator, but a kind of lineage head, to whom both spiritual and secular problems are brought for advice and resolution..., a type of community head, a general factotum".[2] Thus AICs have their own ministry, an authentic and indigenous one, which corresponds to their story, even if this ministry does not conform to the patterns emerging from the theological debates and historical developments in the churches elsewhere.

The authentic African-ness of the AICs is most clearly demonstrated in their style of worship. Since a large proportion of their constituency is non-literate, worship becomes an extremely important tool for forging their life together as a community of faith, a vital and effective instrument for the formation and education of the people. Their worship makes use of genuine African music, the music flowing from the natural rhythms of the words. It is this reality that charged the atmosphere in the service at the Cathedral Church of Christ the King in Cape Coast which we described in chapter 1.

AICs are indigenous for another important reason – that they endeavour to address the hopes and fears of Africans.

Hence their seeming preoccupation with witchcraft and exorcism; and, in regions where racism and political oppression have been the scourge of peoples, they have offered political liberation of a sort.

Archbishop John M. Kivuli II observes that the founding of AICs "was the result of many factors – political, sociological, economic and to an extent physical. In the case of the African Israel Nineveh Church, the aim of the founder, High Priest Paul David Zakayo Kivuli (1896-1974), was to preach the gospel in a way applicable to the local people's situation. This meant developing new traditions in the church."[3]

Within the genre of AIC, the multiplicity of motivations to which Kivuli alludes means that there is great variety. This diversity is indicated by the different type names which have been used to characterize them. It should be noted that a single AIC may belong to more than one type.

Syncretistic movement

Obviously this is not a self-description of the AICs; rather, it is a designation of them by others, quite often intended critically. The characterization of AICs as syncretistic originates in Bengt Sundkler's early attempt to identify them as "the bridge over which Africans are brought back to heathenism",[4] though his later studies abandoned such terminology. The perceived syncretism, the mixing or fusing of Christianity and African traditional religion and practices, is most frequently identified in the use of African music and the embrace by *some* AICs of polygamy, which historic churches officially disallow (even if several of their members actually practise polygamy on the quiet).

The language of syncretism not only confuses issues but is completely oblivious to how the church has acted from its very beginnings. The fourth gospel is a typical example of the style of the early church. Its *exordium* (John 1:1-14) did not invent the word *Logos*. Rather, the author borrowed a word which was very much in use in the books of the Platonists to designate the divine order as the rationality of the universe, the principle of its coherence. One of the great

African Christian thinkers, St Augustine of Hippo, put the point as follows. While admitting the gospel's borrowing from the Platonists, he goes on: "But that 'he came to his own and his own received him not, but that to as many as received him, he gave the power of becoming sons [and daughters] of God to those who believed in his name' – I do not read that there... Again, that the Word was made flesh and dwelt among us, I did not read there" (*Confessions*, Book 7, chapter 9). The point is that the fourth gospel took over what already existed in the culture and thought forms of its addressees *but made something new of it*. Mission starts where people are, with the worldview which they have taken in, so to speak, with their mother's milk. It engages their hopes and fears, builds on them, criticizes them and never tires of setting the transcendent before them.

Against this background we would appeal for the abandonment of the loaded and emotive term "syncretism". In any case, mission which is relevant will have to engage in intercultural translation and interpretation. The New Testament used the ideas and language of the Hebrew and Graeco-Roman context to capture the essential gospel. The use of *Logos* by the fourth gospel was borrowed from the Neo-platonists and reinterpreted. The Christian celebration of Christmas took over much from rites connected with the pagan cult of Thor. Robert Schreiter puts his finger on the issue: the contextualization of the gospel for real persons with a real soul and heart:

> If contextuality is about getting to the very heart of the culture, and Christianity is taking its place there, will not the Christianity that emerges look very much like a product of that culture...? Are we going to continue giving cultures the equivalent of an artificial heart – an organ that can do the job the culture needs, but one that will remain forever foreign?[5]

So our protest against the pejorative use of "syncretistic" to characterize AICs is both a warning against judgmental language and a reminder to the historic churches of a fact of history: that culture has always been the solvent of religion.

Witchcraft eradication movement

This description has sometimes been applied to AICs because of their perceived preoccupation with the overcoming of witchcraft. The early missionaries to Africa tended to deny the reality of witches and to dismiss belief in witchcraft as a remnant of heathenism and superstition. This is not the place for a detailed excursus on the terms heathenism and superstition; others have done such an exercise, including Bolaji Idowu.[6]

The important point for our purposes is that the issue of witchcraft goes to the heart of the African psyche. African societies, like the biblical-Semitic world, have a religious and spiritual understanding of reality. We are surrounded by hosts of spirit beings – some good, some bad – which are considered able to influence the course of human lives. For that reason calamities are attributed to personal forces of evil. In such a setting it is an important role of religion to help free humanity from the tyranny of those forces of evil. It is useless to debate the reality of such spirit beings. Educationally and psychologically it is wise to start from where the addressees are and to travel with them. In any case, whatever the philosophical issues at stake, the thinking of traditional Africa appears to be not dissimilar to what we read in the New Testament: that "our struggle is not against enemies of flesh and blood, but against the rulers, against the authorities, against the cosmic powers of this present darkness, against the spiritual forces of evil in the heavenly places" (Eph. 6:12). In this sense, AICs remind us of a part of the apostolic tradition which the historic churches have tended to try to explain away. AICs thus not only address the hopes and fears of Africans, but also raise the issue of the interpretation of Scripture.

Separatist churches

AICs have also been described as separatist churches. At one level, this is simply an historical observation: that they have often come out of other churches, especially the historic churches. In 1890 some 600 worshippers of St Paul's Breadfruit Church (CMS) in Lagos broke away to establish the

African Church, Lagos. Their protest was against the arrogance of Bishop Herbert Tugwell and the racism perceived in the way the CMS missionaries treated James Johnson, later bishop and one of the stalwarts of the Ethiopianist movement. Jacob Kehinde Coker, one of the founders of this AIC, declared that they "decided to establish the African Church, in which Africans would worship God as Africans, independently, both in spirit and in truth, applying Christianity to African customs, not repugnant to Christ's teachings".[7] If one sees Anglicanism as the English minting of the "one holy, catholic and apostolic church", did these Nigerian Christians not have a legitimate *prima facie* case for their separation?

Similarly, the Church of the Lord (Aladura) separated from the CMS in Nigeria. Interestingly, they saw themselves as a prayer circle which is what the word "Aladura" means – and for their desire to pray meaningfully and as Africans, they were forced out. Thus while it is true that they separated from Anglicanism, Aladura was first and foremost concerned to be a movement to renew African people through Christian teaching.

In Kenya, Matthew Ajuoga founded the Church of Christ in Africa in 1959 after a conflict with the Anglican mission. The conflict had arisen with the publication of the Bible in the Luo language in 1953. That translation rendered the Greek word *philadelphia* (brotherly love) with the Luo term *hera*. Picking up this word, Ajuoga said that the missionaries' treatment of Africans reflected anything but *hera*. When the leadership would not hear his cry, he broke away. Here, too, was separation in search of reform and renewal.

This designation of AICs as separatist is in effect an acknowledgment that they represent a sundering of the one body of Christ and therefore constitute an ecumenical challenge.

Prophetic movement

Some AICs centre on a charismatic teacher and therefore stress religious awakening; hence the designation "prophetic".

An example is *Apostolwo Fe Dede Fia Hiabobo Nun-timya* (Apostle Revelation Society), Tadzevu near Keta, Volta Region, Ghana.[8] It was established in 1939 by Prophet Wovenu, who had been a member of the Ewe (later Evangelical) Presbyterian Church, which grew out of the work of the Bremen Mission in Eastern Ghana beginning in 1847. The faith of this group, so far as we can discern, is by and large the same as that of the Evangelical Presbyterian Church, a member church of the WCC, with some emphasis on the church functioning as a community and on the bonds of solidarity among the members.

In Southern Africa several prophetic movements have arisen. One is the African Apostolic Church of Johane Maranke (AACJM), known popularly among the Shona as *vaPostori* (Apostles). The visions and calling of Johane Maranke are codified in *Umboo utsva hwa-vaPostori* ("The New Revelation of the Apostles"), in which he is identified with biblical leaders, especially Joseph and Moses. The visions are about his receiving special commissions from God. Thus, for example, on 17 July 1932 Maranke, in an experience of the outpouring of the Holy Spirit, heard: "You are John the Baptist, an apostle. Go forth and do my work. Go to every country, preach and convert the people. Command man not to commit adultery, steal or become angry. Baptize people and observe the sabbath!" The important thing to note is the close linkage of prophecy to pastoral work.

Other significant prophets are William Wade Harris (1865-1929),[9] whose legacy is the Twelve Apostles Church, located in Ghana, Ivory Coast and Liberia, and Joseph Babalola and Garrick Braide of Nigeria. At the time the Harris group came into being, a missionary conference in La Zoute, Belgium, was lamenting missionary failures. It is gratifying to note that the conference took note of Harris as "Africa's most successful evangelist", and some taking part expressed the wish that Harris had been present at La Zoute.

It is not without interest to recall some words from the *Lagos Weekly Record* of 18 November 1916:

The God of the Negro, it would seem, has arisen as a strong man from a deep sleep and surveying the wreck and ruin – the physical and moral degradation of the dusky sons of Africa – has gathered up his loins together to redress the balance of the old regime and already has begun to raise up instruments of his sweet will. Prodigies like Garrick or William Waddy Harris are neither impostors nor false prophets. They are merely temporary vehicles for some manifestations of the divine will.

Whatever European missionaries may have said about these prophet movements, Africans took them seriously.

Nativistic churches

This term has been applied to some AICs because they were seen as committed to taking seriously and honouring indigenous life and cultures in communicating the gospel. This signals the heightened sense of pride in race, nation or tribe on the basis of which these churches sought to purge themselves of foreign influences. Examples are the National Church of Nigeria, the Church of Orunmila in Nigeria, the Herero Church of South West Africa (Namibia) and the Bantu Ngqika-Ntsikane Church.

Obviously the term "nativistic" is not their own self-designation, but has been applied to them by others. Unfortunately, the root word "native" has acquired the negative and derogatory connotations of primitive and barbarous; thus, this designation is better not used.

Messianic movement

Some scholars have designated AICs a messianic movement because they were deemed to have strong messianic expectations. The Messiah in this case is not Jesus of Nazareth but the leader of the group. Such alleged Black Messiahs have included Lekhayane of the Zion Christian Church and Isaiah Shembe of the Nazarene Baptist Church of South Africa.

Bengt Sundkler introduced this designation and was followed by G.C. Oosthuizen, Marie-Louise Martin and P. Beyerhaus.[10] Sundkler suggested that the messianism of

such groups was "a radical distortion of prophetically ori-
ented Christianity, as a result of which the Christ of the
Bible was more or less superseded".[11] Other scholars have
suggested that it is the socio-political realities of particular regions of Africa, especially racism and excessive
political oppression, which have spawned such developments.[12]

The attribution of messianism to these churches can be
seen as an *etic* approach to other people's faith. Rather
than engage in long argumentation here, we would
observe that the most eloquent comment on this is the way
in which Sundkler and Martin, on the basis of years of
involvement with them, revised their views.[13] Later,
Sundkler proposed to speak of "iconic" rather than "messianic" leadership: in other words, the prophet is a reflec-
tion and concretization of Christ without necessarily
usurping Christ's place.[14]

But the debate about the designation of this group of
churches points to a more fundamental issue, namely Christ's
mediatorship. Does according such a position to an African
leader minimize the revelation of Jesus? In other words,
there are Christological issues at stake when we encounter
AICs. Some have stated the issue as a question of the role of
the religious leader at the gates of heaven. Daneel is on the
right track when he writes that the iconic leadership "must be
regarded as a projection of a common social usage into the
unknowable realm of life after death, namely the custom that
an ordinary man must never approach an eminent person
except through the agency of an officially sanctioned inter-
mediary".[15]

Spiritual or Pentecostal churches

Pentecostalism is not something peculiar to Africa; as a
phenomenon it has swept through the whole world this cen-
tury – the USA, South America, particularly Chile and
Brazil, South and East Asia, even Europe. Already in 1915
George Jeffrey founded the Elim Four Square Gospel
Alliance. This genus of church movement has a commitment

to experience the Day of Pentecost anew in their time and place. In particular they emphasize the gift of speaking in tongues as being of the *esse* of Christian life and experience.

Some of this tradition percolated into Africa, and certain Pentecostal churches on the continent are patterned after US Pentecostal bodies. But other Pentecostal churches in Africa do not have their origins in Europe or the Americas but reflect an African dissatisfaction with a Christianity that is too cerebral and does not manifest itself in acts of power in the Spirit and Spirit possession. For Africans have a spiritual and religious epistemology and ontology. The Musama Disco Christo Church (MDCC) of Ghana is one example of the home-grown spiritual church.

Others would classify AICs into two broad categories, the Spirit-type and the Ethiopian type. The former have a central focus on the work of and experience of the Holy Spirit, manifested in prophecies, baptism and faith-healing. Among them are the Zionist, apostolic and prophetic types of churches, such as Zion Christian Church of Bishop Mutende in the Shona district of Zimbabwe. The Ethiopian churches are non-prophetic and often claim ideological and religious links with the state of Ethiopia, which becomes the symbol of black people everywhere. Among these are the Chibarirwe African Congregational Church founded by Sengwayo and the African Reformed Church founded by Rev. Sibambo.

Again the various types are not mutually exclusive. For example, Baëta wrote of the Musama Disco Christo Church that it was

> the "spiritual church" with the most pronounced interest in customary practices and national politics in Ghana today [the 1960s]. The present Akaboha [John Appiah II, d. 1974] relates how his father, having predicted that independence would eventually come to the country but not through the Aborigenes' Rights Protection Society, was deluged with enquiries from his followers at the time Dr Kwame Nkrumah started to canvass for support. People wanted to know whether the latter was the person whom the prophecy envisaged, and even more at the time

of the general elections, some members would write in for spiritual consultation, in order to be advised how to cast their vote in the best interests of the country.[16]

Studies indicate that AICs play varied socio-political, economic and religious roles in rural and urban environments. What is clear is that they represent the search of African peoples for a place to feel at home and where they have a sense of belonging.[17]

The language of spiritual, Pentecostal and prophetic leads us to mention also the description of AICs as charismatic. This highlights their emphases on prophecy, healing, prayer and holiness. All such terms put the spotlight on inner renewal and personal well-being, rather than on institutional structures and administrative forms. They seek both inner renewal and African ways to express that renewal. As Sanneh puts it, "biblical material was submitted to the regenerative capacity of African perception and the result would be Africa's unique contribution to the story of Christianity".[18]

We have been hinting that the AICs in their variety belong to a movement, just as the church in its origins was a movement. A movement by definition requires many different voices. The success of the church, especially following its establishment under Emperor Theodosius I, has had the effect of dulling its awareness as a movement. The AICs constitute a reminder to the historic churches that the *status quo* must change. The fact that historic churches are losing their members to AICs underscores the message that change must be on the way.

The varied names applied to AICs indicate the extent of the scholarship which has been devoted to this movement. We may identify three points at which there was a breakthrough. The first was the studies of Sundkler and Efraim Andersson, which made research on AICs a topic of interest. Earlier, they had either been lampooned or dismissed out of hand. Sundkler's study had the other merit of recognizing that not all AICs were of one type, and he distinguished between Ethiopian and Zionist churches.

The second breakthrough was the detailed study by Harold Turner of the Church of the Lord (Aladura). This was a detailed and sympathetic study, moving away from the usual style of polemics. The third breakthrough came with the study under the auspices of the International Missionary Council, which resulted in Hayward's publication *African Independent Church Movements*. Turner and Hayward tightened the language used about the phenomenon of AICs and recognized this movement as definitely Christian.

Let us dwell a little longer on the AICs' search for African identity in the church, looking again at the strong accent on the reality of the Holy Spirit in everyday life.

This emphasis makes sense in a society which understands reality in holistic terms and sees life in terms of a spiritual warfare. In West Africa there is currently an upsurge of what is called gospel music. One such piece of music by Helena Rabbles of Ghana captures in Pidgin English the mood and emphases of African Christianity.

Satan, you don fall ground, O Macha macha
you don fall for gutter
eh! ih! you don fall for ditch, O kwatakwata
Satan I hate your name
Satan, you be trouble maker
Jesus, he go face you now
With one blow, he settle that
O man de tell am
Na you dey cause am
abortions na you dey cause
armed robbery na you dey cause
I hate you, I don't like your name
Jesus don beat you
two thousands years ago
he don beat you again, O Macha macha
Satan, you don fall for ground Oh!
You don fall for gutter Oh! You don fall for ditch Oh!

The English translation is as follows:

Satan you have already fallen
you have fallen into the drain
Hey! you have fallen completely into a ditch
Satan, I hate your name
Satan, you are a trouble-maker
Jesus will face up to you now in a contest
With a blow, he will settle the whole issue
People are saying that
you are the cause of the fight
For you have been behind abortions caused by people
You have been behind armed robbery
I hate you, your very name is an abomination to me
Jesus has already defeated you
two thousand years ago
He has already defeated you thoroughly
Satan, you have already fallen to the ground
you have already fallen down a drain
you have already fallen into a ditch.

The message of this song is that the everyday struggles and troubling experiences of life – whether an abortion or an armed robbery – are manifestations on the human plane of the cosmic battle between the forces of Jesus and those of Satan. Two thousand years ago Jesus won a decisive victory, and it is clear that he will continue to win.

Another illustration of this consciousness of the presence of the Spirit is found in what we may call the Milingo phenomenon.[19] In 1969 at the age of 39 Emmanuel Milingo was appointed archbishop of Lusaka in the Roman Catholic Church of Zambia. In 1982 he was obliged by the Vatican to leave this post, and later he was called to live in Rome away from his native country. The issue in this case was Milingo's ministry of healing in the power of the Holy Spirit, which he began in 1973. Reportedly he healed a woman with physical and mental disorders by inspiration and hypnosis. As he put it, through intense prayer he was "able to reach her soul" to free her from Satan's possession and cure her. Milingo was critical of Christian theologians who operate with a Western frame of reference and whose "ignorance of him [Satan] has even succeeded to subject most of them to himself. They have unknowingly become his agents... In many ways they have nicely misguided the Church through their scientific and systematic theology."[20] While we may not approve of using such language of theological opponents, we should recognize that Milingo's stance reflects the psyche of many Africans who are dissatisfied with how Christianity and Christian theology have been expressed in Africa.

Milingo was hardly the first African theologian to express Christianity in terms of the struggle between Christ and Satan and to feel a yearning to experience the power of the Spirit of Christ in concrete acts of healing and liberation from Satan. Egyankaba Jehu Appiah, founder of the Musama Disco Christo Church was chased out of the Methodist Church of the Gold Coast for "occultism" – practising healing by prayer and in the Spirit. Unlike Jehu Appiah, Simon Kimbangu and others, Milingo has not left his church; and in Rome where he now lives he is very much present in charismatic circles and continues to promote healing by prayer and the Spirit. This indicates that whatever typically African elements may be in the Milingo phenomenon, there is also a link with contemporary charismatic approaches and yearnings elsewhere, including among Europeans and North Americans.

Milingo, like many of the AICs, may be dismissed as a sheer fundamentalist with anti-scientific convictions. But we cannot ignore the fact that the position they take is not unlike the worldview of Jesus and the writers of the New Testament. Kwame Bediako has written:

It is clear from Milingo's ministry and writings that he develops his theological ideas on healing, exorcism and pastoral care consciously in relation to the thought-patterns, perceptions of reality and the concepts of identity and community which prevail within the primal worldview of African societies. He does this, however, not as a mere practical convenience, but because he considers that the spiritual universe of the African primal world does offer valid perspectives for articulating Christian theological commitment.[21]

Whatever our criticisms of Milingo, we would submit that he and the African Christian Initiatives which reflect a Pentecostalist tradition in their stress on encounters with and experience of the Holy Spirit are projecting a sense of mission that is a grappling with the realities of the spiritual world, and of authority and communion with God based on absolute confidence in having received a gift from God through Christ.

In an earlier chapter we made a plea for an *emic* approach to our conversations with AICs. Let us return briefly to this point. The way in which the historic churches speak of AICs often proceeds from the assumption that it is the AICs which are the problem. The designations we surveyed above demonstrate how *etic* interpretations of the phenomenon have shaped even the way in which AICs are described. We have mentioned that in 1948 the Swedish missiologist Bengt Sundkler spoke of them as reflecting a return to heathenism. His *etic* description was followed by G.C. Oosthuizen and Marie-Louise Martin. Happily Sundkler later revised his earlier opinion.

Not only are *etic* approaches unconducive to healthy ecumenical debate, but they also tend to close off attention to a deeper issue of ecclesiology which the unavoidable presence of AICs in world Christianity obliges us to revisit: that of the tests of being church. Theologians of the Reformed tradition will all too quickly resort to their *notae ecclesiae* – preaching of the Word, sacraments and discipline – to resolve the issue. Roman Catholics and Anglicans will apply the criteria of "one holy, catholic and apostolic". But should not the point of ecumenical dialogue be: do we have a right to use our *notae ecclesiae* to judge Christian expressions outside our tradition? Should our time-honoured definitions and creeds and statements of belief have preference over the three cornerstones of religion – namely belief, ritual and religious experience – as means of determining the fidelity of others to the tradition of the church? In this connection we note the judgment offered in Harold Turner's classic study of the Church of the Lord (Aladura): that though this church is "devoid of theological or historic understanding", nevertheless, it is African, yet universal, possessing the notes of the true church "similar to the historic creeds and formulations".[22]

Given the varied designations, what might be identified as the main characteristics of this phenomenon of AIC? We would mention first of all their emphasis on receiving a conscious experience of the Holy Spirit. In this respect they tend to stress baptism in the Holy Spirit rather than baptism with water and the regeneration of the Holy Spirit. This corresponds well with the religious and spiritual epistemology and ontology of black African peoples, who seem unable to explain reality without reference to religion and spirituality. In the African worldview, manifestations of the Spirit are characterized by manifestations of power and the extraordinary. And so receiving the Spirit in the tradition of AICs is often accompanied by *glossolalia*, inarticulate vocal utterance under the stress of religious excitement. For Africans this also reflects a conviction that human language is an inadequate vehicle for the currents of the Holy Spirit.

Second, AICs have a penchant for healing and exorcism. These are effected by the Holy Spirit, with prayer and laying on of hands. The healing is seen in terms of exorcism; for African societies attribute mishap, evil and ailment to personal forces of evil, like witches and demons. This orientation of AICs gives them great appeal in times of crisis, tragedy, severe illness or mental breakdown. The simple truth is that members of the historic churches also often resort to AICs in periods of crisis. By day they attend the services of historic churches, by night they go to AICs, and usually without any sense of disloyalty. In their mind religion must be effective and emotionally satisfying.

It is true that some within AICs have made excessive claims about their ability to heal by the Spirit. In the process they have adopted a somewhat automatic and magical attitude to healing by the Spirit, as if there were a formula which, if applied, would oblige the Spirit to fulfil the wishes of the people. But such excesses stem from the human capacity to abuse any good thing and need not be attributed to any inherent wrong in AICs.

Third, AICs characteristically insist on personal testimony – typically about one's conversion and belief in the Lord – as a mark of devotion. In a rather literalistic interpretation of Romans 10:9, such testimony or confession is marked by a simplicity and sincerity which are seen as part of the mechanics of salvation. This simplicity contrasts rather sharply with the cumbersome and difficult language of the historic churches. How the historic churches expect a non-literate, unschooled African villager to appreciate the language of the Nicene Creed is beyond our imagination. It is far more useful to express the beliefs of the ancient church in the symbols of the Africans than simply to reproduce the ancient formularies themselves. More importantly, their testimonies bear witness to what things the Lord has done for them, and they tell this aloud so that others may join them in praising God.

One aspect of their simplicity of confession which should not be overlooked is that it is practised by both educated and non-educated alike, by the articulate as well as the inarticulate. Often it is assumed that the clientele of the AICs are the non-literate, the uneducated and the poor. We know professors of archaeology, zoology and indeed political science in the University of Ghana who belong to AICs. Harold Turner refers to the "Oxbridge graduates" in the AICs. The head of the Church of the Lord (Aladura) is an agriculturalist in his own right. So an attitude of dismissing AICs as the religion of the simple and uneducated, besides being irrelevant, is uninformed.

We must revise the earlier view that AICs attract only the economically, politically and emotionally disinherited. The popularity of AICs derives from their character of gaiety, emotional expression and enthusiasm and has little if anything to do with class, status, rank and gender. This is a crucial issue. Historic churches have made a practice of complicating the faith – complicated formulas, complicated theological debate, complicated procedures. What can an African villager make of hymns to the Trinity that use language like "consubstantial, co-eternal, while unending ages run"?

Fourth, AICs are a protest movement, principally against the model of church imposed by the North Atlantic captivity of the Christian faith. One indication is the element of nationalism that characterizes some of them. Sometimes their very names point to this. Thus for example in the 1920s there was at Gomoa Affranse in the Gold Coast the Abibipam Church (*abibi* = black African). It was also known as the African Universal (Orthodox Catholic) Church. Its founder was influenced by Marcus Garvey, who established the Universal Negro Improvement Association and proclaimed a black God as a rallying call to give dignity to oppressed blacks. Garvey expounded his idea of a black God as follows:

> If the white man has the idea of a white God, let him worship his God as he desires. If the yellow man's God is of his race let him worship his God as he sees fit. We, as Negroes, have found a new idea. Whilst our God has no colour, yet it is human to see everything through our own spectacles, and since the white people have seen their God through white spectacles, we have only now started out (late though it be) to see our God through our own spectacles. The God of Isaac and the God of Jacob, let him exist for the race that believes in the God of Isaac and the God of Jacob. We Negroes believe in the God of Ethiopia, the everlasting God, God the Father, God the Son and God the Holy Ghost, the One God of all ages. That is the God in whom we believe, but we shall worship him through the spectacles of Ethiopia.[23]

Roughly there have been two waves of African Christian Independency. The first wave broke from the historic churches in a bid to repudiate European administrative control. But beyond the use of the vernacular, nothing much changed in the content and expression of Christianity. The second wave pursued both administrative independence and ritual adaptation.

In the final analysis no classification of a religious movement can be completely satisfactory. But scholars have discerned three broad categories behind all the designations applied to AICs: (1) *Pentecostal*, that is, devoted to a belief system which postulates an omnipotent Creator God who has the ability to do anything; (2) *millennial*, that is, believing in imminent redemption, for which Revelation 21:1,4 are key texts; (3) *thaumaturgical*, with considerable stress on wonders.

As a movement, the AICs have rediscovered the earliest Christian community's self-understanding as *The Way* (cf. Acts 9:2). For this reason it is not surprising that AICs have time and again been political. For as sociology of religion has established, movements by definition have political implications, because, no matter what their purpose, they affect the allocation of power and influence within a community.[24] So if AICs are judged to be political, they are only being true to form – often over against historic churches which have bought into the culture of the European Enlightenment and its separation of epistemology from ontology and ethics, which has made it possible for them to become accomplices in wicked political actions in apartheid South Africa, Mozambique under Portuguese colonial rule and other African dictatorships. A reading of the rise of Independency in Central Africa particularly displays the role played by the desire to be free of white missionaries. These groups were in reality the forerunners of the independent states, besides attesting to the yearning of *homo africanus* for a religion which embraces all of life and the whole of the day.

It cannot be denied that some AICs have been coopted by governments to drum up support in their own power games, as was the case in Ghana under Kwame Nkrumah and under General Acheampong.[25] Moreover, secular leaders have sometimes conferred respectability on spiritual claimants to social leadership. In so doing, governments have used some of them as a counterweight to historic churches and Christian councils.

The reasons that AICs come into being are varied, as this chapter has made evident. However, we may usefully conclude with a summary by J.W. Claasen:

> African believers questioned the condemnation by missionaries of the ancestor cult, circumcision and polygamy. European scepticism with respect to spirit-possession alienated black church members, who found biblical evidence for their view. Their accommodation of African culture made AICs very attractive. The lack of opportunities for African leadership and Western denominations were other causes. The emergence of AICs represented a reaction to conquest, a reaction to European domination in politics, economics, social and church life. Africans sought to create their own institutions free of white control.[26]

NOTES

[1] John S. Pobee, "African Spirituality", in Gordon S. Wakefield, ed., *Dictionary of Spirituality*, London, SCM Press, 1983, p.6.

[2] *Ibid.*

[3] John M. Kivuli II, "The Modernization of an African Independent Church", in Stan Nussbaum, ed., *Freedom and Interdependence*, Nairobi, OAIC, 1984, p.58.

[4] Bengt Sundkler, *Bantu Prophets in Southern Africa*, London, Oxford U.P., 1948.

[5] R.J. Schreiter, *Constructing Local Theologies*, Maryknoll NY, Orbis, 1985, p.150.

[6] Cf. E. Bolaji Idowu, *African Traditional Religion: A Definition*, London, SCM Press, 1973, esp. pp.108-34.

[7] Coker Papers, Files 4/1/28, p.112.

[8] *Apostolwo Fe Dede Fia Hiabobo Nuntimya 1939-1954*, Cape Coast, Mfantisiman Press, 1954; James W. Fernandez, "Rededication and Prophetism in Ghana", *Cahiers d'Etudes Africains*, Vol. 10, no. 2, 1970, pp.228-303.

[9] G.M. Haliburton, *The Prophet Harris: A Study of an African Prophet and His Movement in the Ivory Coast and the Gold Coast 1913-15*, London, Longman, 1975; cf. David Shank, *A Prophet for Modern Times: The Thought of William Wade Harris, West African Precursor of the Reign of Christ*, unpublished Ph.D. thesis, Aberdeen, 1980.

[10] Sundkler, *op. cit.*; cf. Marie-Louise Martin, *The Biblical Concept of Messianism and Missionism in Southern Africa*, Morija, 1964; G.C. Oosthuizen, *Post-Christianity in Africa: A Theological and Anthropological Study*, London, C. Hurst, 1968; P. Beyerhaus, "Begegnungen

mit messianischen Bewegungen", *Zeitschrift für Theologie und Kirche*, Vol. 64, 1967.

[11] Sundkler, *op.cit*, p.323.

[12] Cf. G. Balandier, "Messianismes et Nationalismes en Afrique Noire", *Cahiers Internationaux de Sociologie*, Vol. 14, 1953, pp.41-65.

[13] For Sundkler, see *Zulu Zion and Some Swazi Zionists*, London, Oxford U.P., 1976; for Martin, *Kimbangu: An African Prophet and his Church*, Oxford, Blackwell, 1975.

[14] *Zulu Zion*, pp.193, 310.

[15] Daneel, *Quest for Belonging*, p.191.

[16] C. Baëta, *Prophetism in Ghana*, p.62.

[17] Cf. M.L. Daneel, *Old and New in Southern Shona Independent Churches: Background and Rise of the Major Movements*, The Hague, Mouton, 1971; M.L. Daneel, "Shona Independent Churches in a Rural Society", in J.A. Dachs, ed., *Christianity South of the Zambezi*, Gweru, Zimbabwe, Mambo Press, 1973, pp.159-88.

[18] Lamin Sanneh, *West African Christianity: The Religious Impact*, Maryknoll NY, Orbis, 1990, p.180.

[19] Cf. Emmanuel Milingo, *The World in Between*, London, C. Hurst, 1984; *The Demarcations*, Lusaka, 1981; A. Shorter, *Jesus and the Witchdoctor: An Approach to Healing and Wholeness*, London, Geoffrey Chapman, 1985.

[20] Emmanuel Milingo, *Healing*, n.p., 1976, p.21.

[21] Kwame Bediako, *Christianity in Africa: The Renewal of a Non-Western Religion*, Maryknoll NY, Orbis, 1995, pp.19-23.

[22] Harold W. Turner, *African Independent Church*, 2 vols, London, Oxford U.P., Vol. 2, 1962, p.362. See also W.F. Shenk, "The Contribution of the Study of New Religious Movements to Missiology", in A.F. Walls and W.F. Shenk, eds, *Exploring New Religious Movements*, Indiana, Mission Focus, 1990, pp.194.

[23] *The Philosophy and Opinions of Marcus Garvey*, ed. Amy Jacques, New York, Atheneum, 1969, p.44.

[24] On this see Jan van Baal, "The Political Impact of Prophetic Movements", *Internationales Jahrbuch für Religionssoziologie*, Vol. 5, 1969, p.68.

[25] See John S. Pobee, *Religion and Politics in Ghana*, Accra, Asempa, 1991, pp.76-103.

[26] J.W. Claasen, "Independents Made Dependents: African Independence Churches and the Government", in *Journal of Theology for Southern Africa*, 1991.

5. The Ecumenical Significance of AICs

The incredible growth of Christian churches in Africa is an axiom in contemporary theological-missiological studies. But the equation of the growth of African churches with the vitality of African Christianity is sometimes rather facile. Several African churches, particularly those descended from Western Christian missionary activity, have retained the mental and ministerial bonds of the West. The AICs remind us that Christ would be an African too and that the Euro-American constructs of the gospel are neither satisfying to Africans nor to the whole face of Christ in the world.[1] The church catholic is more than the sum total of the so-called historic churches, be they Latin or Greek.

Notwithstanding the precarious nature of religious statistics, we may be quite sure, on the basis of considerable research over the years, that in the world as a whole and in Africa there is considerable adherence to religion. It is in that context of general religiosity that the AICs are to be located. What seems to be the case with respect to membership is that AICs are outgrowing the historic churches in Africa. Thus A. Anderson is correct in insisting that the study of AICs "is a vital component in the preparation for mission, particularly in Africa. It is no longer a minor and somewhat inconsequential area in the field of missiology, but one of the most important components of religious and theological education today."[2]

The implications of AICs for social life, social change and modernization, especially in the process of urbanization in much of Africa, hardly need to be mentioned. Their significance as a protest movement, whether in terms of inculturation, cultural revival or political action, has also been a very live issue. In Eastern Africa they have taken the form of a prophetic and charismatic movement, led by such persons as John Chilembwe of Malawi, Alice Lenshina in Zambia and Simon Kimbangu in the Belgian Congo – subsequently Zaïre and now the Democratic Republic of the Congo.

In 1981 the WCC sub-unit on Renewal and Congregational Life held a consultation in Kinshasa on ecumenical spirituality in collaboration with the Kimbanguist Church.

After that consultation Walter Hollenweger wrote to the WCC staff responsible for the meeting:

> If the political and social ministry of the Kimbanguists, their prayer-cum-work approach to all economic and social problems, is at least one possible and viable approach for the appalling economic problems of our world, then one would expect the WCC to study this approach and to reflect it in their interchurch aid programmes, in their development programmes, and – last but not least – in their approach through the Commission of Churches on International Affairs (CCIA). We cannot marvel at what the Kimbanguists do and then go home and continue business as usual. Either they have something to contribute which we neglected so far, or they are thoroughly underdeveloped and inefficient and should on this base be told of this evaluation.[3]

We are not convinced that the WCC has in fact creatively explored the implications of that consultation for its own work. Perhaps the jubilee of the Council and its 50th anniversary can be an occasion for resolving to begin taking up this agenda. Several of the comments in Hollenweger's letter point to elements which many Africans find lacking in the minting of the gospel and church which they have inherited from Europe and North America. For the WCC, the central question is what Hollenweger's phrase "prayer-cum-work" says about its own style of operation.

Another participant in the consultation, Michael Harper, a British Anglican priest and a member of the Charismatic Renewal Movement, concluded that Kimbanguists "have much to teach us, particularly about forgiveness and love in the face of persecution, church growth, the place for economic development in the life of a church in a poor country (they are actually involved in development projects, particularly agriculture) and a church's relationship to the state (in the case of Zaïre a repressive dictatorship)".[4] Recently, many have watched with fascinated admiration the post-apartheid South African adventure with the Truth and Reconciliation Commission. Some South Africans have also raised questions about it. Whatever our assessment, alongside that we should not lose sight of the proven experience of the Kim-banguist Church in respect of "forgiveness and love in the face of persecution".

These comments and the continuing relevance of a WCC consultation nearly 20 years ago confirm that AICs like the Kimbanguist Church have their own place in the ecumenical movement and a contribution to make to it. But what are some of the offerings that they make to the historic churches?

First, AICs remind us by their very presence of the complex nature of reality, and therefore of the need to be mindful that our understandings and expressions of that reality are not the only ones, so that in the very nature of the case we must look for complementary ideas and styles of expressing the one truth. In the letter cited above Hollenweger also writes:

> Reality is expressed in culturally contradictory forms. Once that is accepted, we have to make serious concessions concerning other theological categories, like *vere deus* (truly God), *vere homo* (truly human), the trinitarian doctrine and above all the *filioque*. This drives right into the heart of today's theological debate and is an issue with which the charismatic and the ecumenical movements will have to wrestle in future.

There is here a hint that the ecumenical movement's beholdenness to doctrinal criteria is inadequate.

We have spoken earlier of the fissiparous tendency of AICs – their penchant to break up and further subdivide. The reasons for this tendency are many and varied, some of them cultural. Certainly it signals a disruptive element which can undermine the unity of the church and may be symptomatic of a superficial ecclesiology which sees the church as nothing more than a human association. On the other hand, some of the schisms have stimulated church growth, conversion and spiritual renewal. And despite schisms a basic loyalty remains to the spiritual "home", the church family/prophetic movement. That is why once positions have been consolidated after a break, efforts are made to seek meaningful cooperation within the broader family.

The general features of AICs which we mentioned in the previous chapter, while more characteristic of certain AICs than of others, also identify points of potential ecumenical discussion and mutual learning. First, there is emphasis on a conscious experience of receiving the Holy Spirit, with stress put on baptism in the Holy Spirit rather than baptism by water and regeneration of the Holy Spirit. Second, the reception of the Holy Spirit is believed to be accompanied by *glossolalia*. Some would argue that this is an inheritance from the Pentecostal/Charismatic movement. But there is also a particularly African contribution: a spiritual epistemology and ontology which are not satisfied with a heavily rational and materialist approach to religion, and a belief that human language is inadequate for the currents of the Holy Spirit.

The third element we identified is the characteristic stress AICs place on healing and exorcism, effected through the Holy Spirit, prayer and laying on of hands. We have argued that this position of the AICs is consistent with both biblical teaching and practice and African traditional culture. By contrast, the Western-initiated churches have ceded the healing ministry to doctors and hospitals and thus tended to overlook the depth of the healing ministry of Jesus. In the historic churches moral and spiritual healing are provided for sacramentally; but miraculous cures are associated with shrines and saints. Aylward Shorter, a Roman Catholic priest of the religious community of White Fathers, has written:

> The church's own sacramental life appears to have little impact or at least to have little apparent relevance to the multi-dimensional needs of the new Christians in the sphere of suffering and relief from suffering. Existing liturgical and canonical forms make it difficult to incorporate the new healing traditions that are springing up and there is a real danger of heterodoxy or even schism.[5]

In Africa ministry will be judged deficient if it does not treat healing as a function of religion. Here the AICs have brought to the fore a tradition of the church which has been in danger of being lost. Thus AICs pose an ecumenical challenge regarding the wholeness of ministry and theological and ministerial formulas.

AICs by their style represent the spontaneous expansion of the church. The whole church, leadership and all, assume that it is the church's task to multiply, in short to do mission. And they do so through simplicity of confession and simple living and simple Christian witness.

Many adherents of AICs are not into heavy intellectualism, and the heart and dynamic of their vibrant religious life is worship. For this reason any dialogue between AICs and confessional or doctrinal ecumenism will have to zero in on worship. This is not as unlikely as it may sound at first hearing. It is in fact nearer to the experience and practice of the early church, which expressed its faith not so much in propositional statements as in hymns, doxologies, liturgies and prayers.

In 1996 the Organization of African Instituted Churches, the Centre for Black and White Christian Fellowship (Selly Oak Colleges) and the Catholic Fraternity convened a consultation in Nairobi. *Baragumu*, a publication of AICs, devoted an editorial to it. It included this testimony:

> We have, as Christians, unashamedly fought each other in the past. We have dwelt on trivialities at the expense of true mission. The time is now to start praying together without ceasing (Rom. 12:11-13) and to admonish one another with love (Eph. 4:15) until we arrive at the meeting point. The writing is on the wall, bold and clear. We have two options. One is to listen to the loving voice of God and that is to work as a team. The other is to fail to do so and stand condemned for posterity for creating loopholes for hostile religions, cults and fundamentalisms of all shades to eat into the very foundations of the legacy bequeathed to us by our Master Jesus Christ. I doubt whether we have an alternative.[6]

Whatever else it says, this underlines the importance of prayer and worship together as the way forward in realizing the ecumenical imperative.

6. The Problems and Promise of AICs

Though African in origin, AICs today are not confined to Africa. Lively AIC groups can be found, for example, in Amsterdam, London and Birmingham, Hamburg, Geneva and Zurich. Both the Musama Disco Christo Church and the Church of the Lord (Aladura) have had vibrant branches in London for about 30 years. Non-Africans have become members of these churches. Thus what started off as a church for Africans has now opened its doors to Europeans and others. By this opening AICs are becoming not only global and international but also ecumenical and missionary. They can no longer be ignored. The Council of Churches in the Netherlands and churches in Hamburg are beginning to take a closer look at them, not so much to be critical but to discern what may be learned from them.

The thriving reality of AICs in the Netherlands is especially significant. At least 20 AIC congregations are found in Amsterdam alone, and they are making their way to other cities. This is noteworthy in a country which has been described as the most secular in Western Europe. True, quite a few of the members are Africans who have made their way to Holland fleeing expulsions, economic hardship and warfare in their own countries. But these churches have been attracting Dutch members as well. In that sense they are succeeding where historic churches are losing their grasp. The historic churches would do well to take lessons from their apparent success.

AICs are encountered today in the context of a shift in the demography of world Christianity. In the words of Andrew Walls, there is a "complete change in the centre of gravity of Christianity, so that the heartlands of the church are no longer in Europe, decreasingly in North America, but in Latin America, in certain parts of Asia, and most important for our present purposes, in Africa".[1] A significant part of this development is the growing and vibrant presence of AICs. The very fact of their appearance in European cities along with their major share of the growth and vibrancy of African Christianity accords AICs a significance which the ecumenical movement can ill afford to ignore.

The AICs' attractiveness to converts at home and abroad indicates that they are delivering goods that are welcome to the people. This means that they are dispensing a theology that is sufficiently coherent and attractive to make a difference to people. Here a second important observation is in order: the AICs have a theology that is worth talking about because, as Walls says, it has a "noticeable effect on the lives and minds of a significant number of people".[2] The implication of this for the survival of theology and world church hardly needs to be drawn out.

A third quotation from the same essay by Walls is of immediate relevance to an assessment of the ecumenical significance of AICs: "A church catholic implies that the resources of all Christian ages and places are open to uninhibited exploitation by all Christians."[3] The churches of the North and the West can learn from AICs, especially from how they are conducting themselves in a way that leads to growth. But readiness to learn from AICs has hardly been the major response to this striking phenomenon of our time.

One response has been hostility, name-calling and condemnation. Our review of the designations applied to AICs has drawn attention to the *etic* descriptions which often obfuscate the real issues and lead to sharp criticism which fails to engage AICs on their own terms. A milder form of this is to be derisory or make fun of them. This is nothing new: a white Anglican bishop in Nigeria, Melville Jones, responded to secessions from his church which formed the United Native African Church (1891) and the African Church, Bethel (1901) by saying scornfully, "They call themselves 'African', but their services, the robes and titles of their ministers, their surpliced choirs are all borrowed from England... How are they distinctly African?"[4] One may imagine that the bitterness lurking in this response had largely to do with the fact that some of the membership of Jones's own church had gone over to these AICs.

If the hostility of historic churches over membership losses is understandable at one level, it nevertheless risks being a denial of the freedom of people to choose their own faith and the tradition with which they wish to associate. Such an attitude is a subtle assault on religious freedom, freedom of conscience and human rights. Moreover, the hostile response avoids the really vital and significant issue: where have the historic churches failed to do right by their adherents, so that they have decided to desert the historic church and cross over to an AIC? Without facing this fundamental question, the historic churches cannot hold their membership. In that sense, AICs offer an invitation to the historic churches to rethink their understanding of the church and how they are going about their life and business as churches.

A second response is to be neither hot nor cold regarding AICs. Such a response is inadequate for at least two reasons. For one thing it reveals a patronizing attitude which breeds isolation, the opposite of *koinonia*, instead of supporting the fellowship. Second, such an attitude may in effect be sacrificing some truth. Accepting freedom of conscience and freedom of association is not the same thing as treating the ecumenical option like a supermarket of traditions to be taken at will. Deep and sensitive convictions and commitments are at stake; and this brings us to the third response.

The only viable response to the AIC development in our view is to engage them in a dialogue for mutual enrichment, treating the encounter as a learning experience. The AICs concretize for the churches and the ecumenical movement the agenda of *koinonia* which is central to the ecumenical vocation. An ecumenical movement which has held up a basic ecclesiology of *koinonia* should be committed to critical solidarity of all who claim to belong to the one body of Christ. Such solidarity invites all within that body to endeavour to live amicably and respectfully despite differences. Solidarity takes precedence over reservations and cynical interpretations.

AICs are often talked about as though they were a recent phenomenon. In fact, as we have seen, they have been bubbling up since the nineteenth century, although the phenomenon has become more pronounced in our times. Earlier we have referred to Ethiopianism and to the traditions represented by Rufus Anderson and Henry Venn. AICs are building on that yearning of earlier African Christians and missionaries. Tracing the ancestry of AICs to Ethiopianism raises another issue: the call for an independent *non-denominational* African church. A bane of the historic churches is that they are often held in captivity to a founding missionary body or denomination through a system of grants. The idea of the "three-self" has hardly ever been implemented. The grants have been made according to the needs of institutional self-interest and thus have perpetuated denominationalism. Without a vision and sense of mission the model of self-supporting is self-serving and self-perpetuating.

AICs are often said to recruit the poor and excluded and to depend on their meagre resources. But since these churches have no missionary "godfathers" to turn to, they must take responsibility for the entire life, including the financial needs, of their churches. Thus they instill an acute sense of tithing while at the same time not being beholden to any external denominational authorities.

The lesson to be drawn from all this is that a non-denominational church and a viable ecumenical movement in Africa can emerge only when the idea of a moratorium on external personnel and funding has been given cash value. By the same token, the temptation for AICs to look outside for financial support must be carefully assessed. Indeed, various meetings of AICs have devoted attention to the issue of partnership and dependence, focusing particularly on how to prevent the relationship between AICs and mission churches from degenerating into dependency on non-African resources. In this way an authentic interdependence may be discovered.

AICs are a contemporary attempt to realize *in their own way* the three-self principle. Precisely because they were self-founding – in the sense of not being the result of any initiative by foreign missionaries or mission boards – AICs have automatically become self-governing, self-supporting and self-propagating. Stan Nussbaum has suggested that instead of focusing on the criterion of self-supporting, which concentrates on finances, we should speak of the more dynamic concept of self-*motivating*: "Motivation causes things to move rather than simply to stand still. A self-motivating church is driven by its past experience of God's action and pulled towards the work it is called to do."[5] Instead of self-propagating we might substitute self-*contextualizing*, focusing on the quality of the message and the whole identity of the church. We could further replace self-governing by self-*critical*. Such a quality highlights the need for openness to prophetic voices in how affairs are conducted, with mission rather than maintenance of the structure as the overriding concern.

Thus even if AICs are seen as representing the tradition initiated by Rufus Anderson and Henry Venn and Ethiopianism, they have moved on to see the key criteria of mission in a revised three-self formula: self-motivating, self-contextualizing and self-critical. The historic churches can learn from this. In Nussbaum's words:

> The African Independent Churches have exposed the limits of the old three-self formula by achieving it without being complete models of mature churches. Their pioneering experiences after achieving it are experiments at the cutting edge of mission which point us towards a restatement of the three-self formula: self-motivating, self-contextualizing and self-critical.[6]

Their experiment is not complete but they are pressing on in the right direction.

In part the rise of AICs may be understood in terms of a power vacuum that has resulted from the transition from mission church to independent historic church. In many cases the withdrawal of missionaries left behind an African leadership that could not fulfil the aspirations of the faithful, not to mention the drying up of resources in the form of financial aid from abroad. This new situation led to much strife and schism. The issue is how to manage the power vacuum so that it does not generate further divisions in the one holy, catholic and apostolic church.

A striking recent phenomenon has been the rise of associations of AICs. Perhaps the best known is the Organization of African Instituted Churches (OAIC), headquartered in Nairobi, Kenya. In Ghana there has been the Pentecostal Association of Ghana, most of whose members were founded in Ghana and have no foreign origins or connections. Other groupings in Ghana are the National Council of Pentecostal Churches, the Ghana Council of United Churches and the Christian Brotherhood Council. Tragically, there has been no love lost among these groupings themselves.

In 1972 Fambidzano no yamaKereke avaTema – the African Independent Churches Conference – was established among Shona independent churches. Today it has more than 50 member churches. The significance of the Fambidzano development is that it points to natural solidarity as a basis for ecumenism. This stands alongside the thinking in institutions like the WCC that convergence on theological disagreements is the way forward to unity. Daneel writes:

> Once it became evident that these churches could uphold their identity, and as ties of friendship were forged through cooperation, the Zionist leaders were able to modify their critical attitude towards the Ethiopian-type churches, which had been in condemnation of the latter's alleged neglect of the Holy Spirit. This did not in itself resolve the doctrinal differences, but it became easier to abandon group prejudices through the establishment of common goals, greater recognition and status and especially the absence of an involved dogmatic-historical background such as besets Western churches. Unity in Christ as defined in John 17:21,23 was made a cornerstone of the Shona ecumenical movement from the outset. The fact that in the early years the Zionist churches were prepared to tolerate a preponderance of leaders of Ethiopian-type churches in the administrative board despite their own numerical superiority indicated an amazing sense of solidarity.[7]

OAIC and Fambidzano were by no means the first attempts at ecumenical cooperation among AICs. Already in 1919 a conference was held in Bloemfontein, South

Africa, with the aim of uniting black clergy and laity. The pioneer in this development was Rev. Mkhize, a Zulu minister. In the 1920s the African National Congress launched the United National Church of Africa, but it did not last long, partly because almost no attention was paid to denominational and doctrinal differences. This experience suggests a significant corrective to the idea of relying solely on natural solidarity. There is no way in which an ecumenical quest can come alive in a divided world if denominational and doctrinal differences are not acknowledged and faced head-on.

Other ecumenical groupings also developed in the region of Southern Africa. In 1937 the Bantu Independent Churches Union of South Africa was initiated to serve the Zulus, but it also proved to be short-lived. In 1939 the AME Church accepted a federation of churches. A conference at Queenstown in 1965 led to the formation of the African Independent Churches' Association (AICA). Between 1965 and 1972 its membership grew from 100 to 400.

We would highlight three motives behind these movements. In the first place, they represented a striving for recognition from both the historic churches and the government. Second, they expressed a smouldering yearning for greater unity among the AICs. Third, they encapsulated a desire for better theological education. Let us dwell a bit more on this last point.

Even though there is some anti-intellectualism and anti-theological sentiment in the historic churches in Africa, a constant criticism they make of AICs is that the latter are not theologically sound, leading to charges of deviations from the true faith. On the other hand, the AICs themselves, even when they stress the gifts of the Holy Spirit, nevertheless emphasize the need for a theological education of sorts. Already in 1965 some AICs negotiated for theological education with the multi-racial and inter-denominational Christian Institute in South Africa. In Zimbabwe Fambidzano has had a thriving Theological Education by Extension (TEE) programme. In Ghana, with the help of the Mennonites in particular, the Good News Institute was set up to facilitate the educational aspirations of AICs. In Nigeria, the Church of the Lord (Aladura) has its own seminary. The Kimbanguist Church has a theological programme, including a theological faculty. The OAIC has had a thriving TEE programme for quite some time. The interest of AICs in theological education has also brought them into contact with the WCC and its programme on Ecumenical Theological Education.

These initiatives in theological education have given AICs standing as churches as well as the advantages of the education itself. It has offered them new perspectives on the development of Christianity, in the process stimulating self-knowledge and self-criticism vis-à-vis other churches and world Christianity. It has moulded the theological thinking of their leadership. In short, AICs have sought ecumenical cooperation on the basis of inherent ecumenical trends within themselves and have put in place constructive measures to counteract the tendency towards schism and individual freedom.

An underlying concern for AICs in this area is: "Do you train a prophet or does a prophet simply arise?" Putting the issue in this provocative form draws attention to the phenomenon of AIC leaders emerging from obscurity one day to the status of prophet the next. Some of these leaders would state quite simply that they have been to the University of the Holy Spirit and therefore do not need any seminary training. Today, however, there is growing appreciation that even those who are seized upon by the Spirit can benefit from some continuing formation.

In some cases, unfortunately, the immediate consequence of sending students to colleges has been to motivate them to branch out of their original denomination and establish their own church, thus adding to the proliferation of churches. This situation must be on the agenda of all engaged in theological and ministerial formation.

Some AICs exemplify the cross-ethnic dimensions of Christian renewal in Africa. A good illustration of this is the

Harrist movement. While its founder was Liberian, it began in Ivory Coast and spread to Ghana. Its membership not only went beyond colonial borders but also put numerous ethnicities into one church. It sought at first to cope with this ethnic diversity through "a comprehensive territorial organization of dioceses and archdioceses with a metropolitan see at Abia-Niambo, complete with cardinals, a sacred college and even a pope".[8] About this experiment Sanneh remarks: "The effort, predictably, failed, for the vernacular ferment was too powerful to reduce to such a uniform mould. Eventually a complex structure was evolved to reflect the pluralistic ethos of the movement."[9] The option for the vernacular paradigm comes with the challenge of pluralism, and it is in the creative engagement of the two that a viable ecumenical spirit can be found.

We may conclude this survey of the ecumenical challenges of AICs by returning to three issues raised earlier: the affirmation of the "one holy, catholic and apostolic church", the Word and the sacraments.

We often forget that the established language of "one holy, catholic and apostolic church" reflects what we may call the "official theology" that emerged from the early centuries when church and empire were bound in one. This process began with the emperor Constantine I (306-337) and continued with Theodosius (379-395) and beyond. Constantine tried to restore the ancient glory of the Roman empire on the basis of Christianity. This was concretized in the Byzantine empire, with its seat in Byzantium and its emperor assuming the right, as "bishop of bishops", to intervene in the life of the church. The official theology equated the peace and unity of the church with the peace and unity of the state or empire. In that context we can see the beginnings of the language which became crystallized as "one holy, catholic and apostolic church". Had history been otherwise, we wonder whether such language would have come to be used of the church. The point here is the influence of contextual factors on the language of church teaching, the interface of theological debate and political intrigue.

Without going into an exposition of the whole phrase, let us look briefly at two of its terms – *one* and *catholic*. "One" easily picks up what has been said above about one empire and one faith. This affirmation was of course regularly put to the test by the controversies of the time, especially in North Africa by the schism of Donatism and the controversy around Arianism. "Catholic" meant universal, pointing to the reality that the one empire had one religion as its cement. But it also came to mean "according to the whole". As Justo González explains:

> To separate itself from the various heretical groups and sects, the ancient church began calling itself "catholic". This title underscored both its universality and inclusiveness of the witness on which it stood. It was the church "according to the whole", that is, according to the total witness of all the apostles. The various Gnostic groups were not "catholic" because they could not claim this broad foundation. Indeed, those among them who claimed apostolic origins did so on the basis of a hypothetical secret tradition handed down through a single apostle. Only the church "catholic", the church "according to the whole" could lay claim to the entire apostolic witness. Ironically, through an evolution that took centuries, debates regarding the true meaning of "catholic" came to be centred on the person and authority of a single apostle – Peter.[10]

Perhaps we invoke the time-honoured phrase "one holy, catholic and apostolic church" in a manner that is too facile to be really helpful in ecumenical debate, especially when we address the place of the AICs in the world church. Can we find other language to capture the essence of what this time-honoured phrase tries to convey?

As for Word and sacrament, the commitment of AICs to the Word is not in dispute. Some would even describe the devotion of AICs to the Bible as radical biblicism, because they encourage Christians to live the Scriptures. What may occasion debate is the interpretation of the Word of God. But that is not peculiar to them; it is an issue also in the historic churches.

Where there is extensive room for debate is around the sacraments. Several commentators have called attention to the place of the eucharist in the Kimbanguist Church in its earliest days. Andrew Walls summarizes it well:

> The sacraments, indeed, have not been a prominent feature of many African Independent Churches, but it is also true that they have not been prominent in African Christianity as a whole. This results from the fact that the mission churches, Catholic and Protestant, have insisted on the practice of their countries of origin, that only a priest or minister is permitted to officiate at the sacrament, and there have never been enough of these to make sacramental worship more than a periodic experience for most African Christians. In some areas a further feature has been that church discipline in conflict with local marriage custom restricts the communion in practice to a minority, often an older minority, of the congregation. It is not surprising if the independents have often taken the sacrament – and the creeds – as something that is part of being a church, part of tradition, but not as something near the heart of religious life. The EJCSK in Zaïre in effect kept the communion service in cold storage for years and then installed it, with great solemnity and an indigenization of the elements. But the communal meal, long prominent in African societies, has blossomed independently of the Eucharist. For instance, South African Zionists will break the Lenten fast with joy and gusto on Easter morning, but without the bread and wine or the words of the institution. The Eucharist came to Africa without emphasis on its aspect as a communal meal, and the Christian communal meal has gone on, in older and independent churches alike, developing without the eucharist.[11]

NOTES

[1] A.F. Walls, "Towards Understanding Africa's Place in Christian History", in John S. Pobee, ed., *Religion in a Pluralistic Society* (Essays presented to Professor C.G. Baëta), Leiden, E.J. Brill, 1976, p.180.

[2] *Ibid.*, p.183

[3] *Ibid.*

[4] Cited in J.B. Webster, *The African Churches Among the Yoruba*, Oxford, Clarendon Press, 1964, p.125.

[5] Stan Nussbaum, "African Independent Churches and a Call for a New Three-Self Formula for Mission", in Nussbaum, ed., *Freedom and Interdependence*, p.2.

7. Quo Vadimus?

The rich variety within the genre of African Initiatives in Christianity means that it is not wise or helpful to make sweeping generalizations about them. What is true of one may not be true of another. An obvious example is plural marriages: some approve them, others do not. We have to learn to take AICs seriously in their individuality.

It is true that AICs have taken their cue from African traditional religions in offering ritual and spiritual remedies to the questions and problems arising for Africans out of their sense of physical and spiritual vulnerability. But it is important to note as Baëta did that the answer the AICs give to this sense of vulnerability is not the traditional resort to many gods and lords, or to charms and amulets. Rather, he says:

> The "spiritual churches" represent a turning away from these traditional sources of supernatural succour in order that help may be sought... from the God proclaimed in the Christian evangel. As the needs, cravings and hopes remain unchanged, so also the basic ideas regarding the character of the universe, of its forces, their possibilities and the modes of their operation have been preserved intact. In point of fact, this turning away "from idols to serve a living and true God" does not appear to be essentially different from the usual practice in African religion whereby a God or fetish which has plainly failed to meet the requirements of its supplicants is abandoned in order that another one, believed to be more effective, may be embraced. The "spiritual churches" indeed have a very strong conviction that at long last the passage has been made from error to truth, from the wrong path to the right one, from darkness to light; and that because this is so, the newly-found resource of helpful power cannot fail.[1]

If this judgment is correct, then we should desist from calling AICs "post-Christian" (cf. Oosthuizen) or castigating them as a return to heathenism. Such judgments are not in the best interests of healthy ecumenical dialogue.

Kwame Bediako, another African scholar, has suggested that AICs offer a paradigm of "the primal imagination". In a study of William Wade Harris, "the first African Christian prophet", he writes: "Prophet Harris appeared to function in a spiritual universe which was both simple and complex, and yet he seemed able to embrace it as a totality. It is this outlook which makes him... a paradigm of... the primal imagination."[2] African churches as a whole need "the primal imagination" which lies at the heart of the AICs, and the ecumenical movement must create space for and engage "the primal imagination".

Taking seriously this "primal imagination" necessarily entails a commitment to the vernacular paradigm of being church. In church history the stories of the Armenian Church and the Gothic tradition confirm this necessity. The ecumenical movement needs to be a space for dialogue between various vernacular paradigms, with none excluded *ab initio*.

The vernacular paradigm means holding two things in tension: the traditions of the one holy, catholic and apostolic church, and the questions and issues arising from the various paradigms, particularly around Scripture, Christ, Holy Spirit, church and ministry. Such a dialogue can happen only if we go slow on resorting to words like "heresy" and "syncretism". They are too often used, and we need rather to be moving in the direction of seeking to see things in complementary terms.

Missionary Christianity has been too much dominated by the intellect. AICs teach us that the proclamation of the gospel should touch both the heart and the mind. If proclamation is for the purpose of transformation of peoples, then emotion must be touched, for only then will change be possible.

We have referred repeatedly to the difficulties caused by the fissiparous dynamics of AICs – their tendency towards splintering. A study of the Bassa Independent Churches of Liberia offers some interesting insights into this problem which may be applied, in varying degrees, to other churches. The Bassa schisms are basically due to four factors.[3] First is leadership. Sometimes the leader of the church, particularly the founder, is tempted to treat the church as his private property. The model of leadership is thus absolute monarchy. This is often resented by younger persons in the church, who then attempt to sweep away such leadership. A second, related factor is financial irregularity. Leadership which is tempted to treat the church as its private property will not resist the temptation to make no distinction between private property and funds and church property and funds; and this will not go on unchallenged forever. A third potential source of schism is church discipline. There are cases in which persons against whom the church takes disciplinary action will simply decide to break away from the church rather than submit to its discipline. Finally, some schisms have been in reaction to missionary control. The stories of Malawi mentioned earlier are an illustration of this.

It is evident that there is nothing peculiarly African about these motivations for schism: they can be found in the experience of churches in every other part of the world as well. But AICs confront some other factors. One is the weight of the sociological heritage. To remain with the Bassa example: the typical village has only about 20 huts. This predisposes the Bassa churches to split rather than grow big.[4] At the same time, changes in the world put a new slant on these fissions. For example, the Pentecostal explosion of the 1980s has brought the idea that establishing a new church, far from wounding the body of Christ, is fulfilling the missionary vocation:

> According to this ecclesiology, the true church is made up of all born-again believers, and has nothing to do with these organized bodies traditionally called churches. To start a new cell of born-again believers is not seen as severing communion with any church, but as a step towards fulfilling the great commission, an act of great virtue, and regarded as such even by those with whom one used to worship. From this perspective, the concept of "split" is not very helpful.[5]

Another change in the factors leading to schisms can be seen in the political context. During the 1960s and 1970s, the initial euphoria of political independence was a motivation for seeking ecclesial independence as well. By contrast, in the 1980s and 1990s the euphoria has evaporated and in many places given way to poverty, pain and disillusionment. An important factor in the schisms is now economic.

The complexities to which we have pointed on the African continent – which are also present in different forms elsewhere – make the ecumenical task extremely complicated. The theological task must be tackled with a keen sensitivity to all these other factors at play. The traditional Faith and Order issues have to be in dialogue with these other factors. Here is a call for a new way of doing theology – one which proceeds by and endeavours to be in dialogue with "all sorts and conditions of humanity", in order to convict them for the one church of God through Jesus Christ.

* * *

In this study we have offered personal views based on our own observations and reflections as well as drawing on the work of a range of scholars, theologians and missiologists. It is appropriate to conclude by listening to AICs speak for themselves, in their own vocabulary and idiom. We shall cite two texts from the Organization of African Instituted Churches: an OAIC Manifesto and their own perception of their contributions to the world church. Both date from 1996, and were published in *Baragumu*, July 1996.

A New Force of Christian Churches
An OAIC Manifesto

"We, the Independent churches, cannot be ignored anymore. Indifference will not make us disappear. The African Independent Churches [are] one of the fastest growing phenomena in the whole world. In fact, we are the fastest growing churches, even more than the Pentecostals in South America. The *World Christian Encyclopaedia* indicates that in South Africa alone there was a total of 6,249,800 in the mid-80s, and expected that to increase to 12,737,000 by the year 2000. The adherents of Independent Churches in Zaïre [Democratic Republic of Congo], where the largest Christian denomination of Africa is the Church of Jesus Christ on Earth through the Prophet Simon Kimbangu, numbered

4,777,500 in mid-1980 and were expected to increase by the year 2000 to 8,848,500.

"The existence of the mushrooming Independent or indigenous churches is due to their decision to discontinue relating or not to relate to mission churches, their missionaries and their structures. Why?

"One main reason is because our leaders felt that the missionary zeal to save souls from eternal damnation with Christianity robed in foreign clothes did not take into account the fact that the Western God was spiritually inadequate and irrelevant to deal with the reality of many aspects of our lives. The result was a Christian faith and conviction which were only 'skin-deep' or superstitious, in spite of the successful spread of Christianity on the continent. There was and is still the question of how deep the Christian faith really is when so many of its affiliates still continue to visit the caretakers of the African traditional religions.

"The Independent Churches were attempts by African Christians to live our Christian faith in our own national garb without an *a priori* theologizing. We sought to establish a Christianity of the Bible as we saw it, without Western additions and in harmony with our own cultural heritage. We attempted to come to grips with the traditional beliefs and practices and worldviews implied; to make the Christian faith come alive to our own thought processes and culture.

"We can also say that African Independent Churches (AICs) – or Spiritual Churches as some of us call ourselves – are African social entities, some of which developed in the context of changes in the relationship between traditional and modern sectors of the larger communities, that is, a social transformation as a reaction to urban society.

"The resulting new belief systems had the idea of a continuity between traditional and modern worldviews, an effort to find new Christian ways of coping with witchcraft, the disintegration of the extended family, urban loneliness and other issues. The AICs served as adoptive and substitute institutions to help us cope with the changing social scene.

"We also developed out of the rising nationalist sentiment, not always actively participating in the political struggle, but responding to an 'African consciousness'. African
values were naturalized into the Christian tradition.

"We African Independent Churches try to live Christianity with our own national clothing, in harmony with our own
cultural heritage, seeking vehicles of worship that make the
Christian faith alive to us as Africans. We have evolved our
own liturgy and hymnology, our own doctrinal emphases. In
yearning for spiritual satisfaction, and psychological and
emotional security, we re-introduced an 'emotional depth'
into Christianity.

"The AICs are the most needy in terms of being the least
educated, the most ridiculed and feared, to the point of some
being persecuted by government decrees outlawing their
existence, as in Togo. Although in many countries many of
us have won the respect of our governments, there is still in
some places a strong pressure from established or historical
churches on their governments to continue this non-recogni-
tion of our existence.

"This happens even when the AICs are the weakest of the
Christian family in terms of vulnerability, and should be
cared for by the strongest."

AIC contributions to the world church

"In spite of the interpretation many in the Western world
give to the AICs, most of us are stable, growing churches
with a Christian doctrine based on the Bible as sole authority, a special dispensation of the Holy Spirit, faith in the God
of the Bible and confidence in its promises. One can say with
conviction that AICs are part of the universal church and
have much to contribute to her life. The following are a few
of our contributions which can enrich the church around the
world:

"1. The AICs have helped the Western church to discover
the secondary or negotiable elements derivative of Western
culture and imported with the gospel into Africa. In other
words, we can now distinguish between the gospel, a univer-

sal gift of God to all humankind, and its Western wrappings. We have revived our culture that had been branded as sinful by missionaries, causing many Africans later to discard Christianity as un-African.

"2. We have helped the mainline churches in developing countries to discover and develop new avenues of being the church in Africa, ceasing to be a missionary or Western church.

"3. We show how a focus upon the world as a whole, both spiritual and material, is possible in contrast to the dichotomous Western worldview that divides the sacred from the profane, the spirit from matter, the supernatural from the natural. Our relationship to God's whole creation is one of respect and gratefulness.

"4. We may not all be articulate in written theology, but we express faith in our liturgy, worship and structures. Our services are alive with warm expressions of joy as we clap and dance in rhythm with the new spiritual and indigenous songs. Needless to say, the people come because they feel at home.

"5. AICs may not be used as agents of political, economic and cultural domination because we have not lost our sense of identity, being aware that the myth 'universal is equal to Western' erodes Christian love and trust among the children of God.

"6. We have contributed to the Christian ideal of diversity in ecumenicity as an example to nations and churches 'to be themselves'.

"7. We awaken themes that have become dormant or latent in the universal church due to the destructive influence of technology and science on relational life, such as:

a. *The wholeness of creation* – the Western world has lost the intuition of the sacred by rejecting symbols which used to connect.

b. *Fecundity* – the generation of life and the sharing of it through interpersonal relationships are emphasized.

c. *Humans-in-community* – we have a spiritual view of life that nourishes our sense of family and community.

d. *Communion of saints* – the relationship between the living and the dead enrich our churches as the living nurture the memory of our predecessors who are still influencing our own lives by their contributions to the welfare of our communities when they were still alive.

e. *The church as a life-giving organ in society* through the influence of its members in the marketplace – because our faith is not a private act, but literally 'carried on our sleeves' or our clothes.

f. *The renewal of the Holy Spirit* is continuous with and greater than the spirits around us. Our dependence on the Holy Spirit for protection from evil forces has liberated us to share with others our freedom from fear, a very enticing proposition in the African context, as well as in the rest of the world.

g. *Spiritual healing*, in most of the AICs, is, in a literal sense, the principal focus of our worship and liturgical practices, being the main cause of our impressive growth."

NOTES

1 C. Baëta, *Prophetism in Ghana*, p.135.
2 Kwame Bediako, *Christianity in Africa*, p.92.
3 Mark Scheffers, "Schism in the Bassa Independent Churches of Liberia", in David A. Shank, ed., *Ministry of Missions to African Independent Churches*, Elkhart, Indiana, Mennonite Board of Missions, 1987, pp.62-95.
4 Perry Tinklenberg, "Christian Extension Ministries of the Christian Education Foundation of Liberia", in Shank, *ibid.*, pp.96-112.
5 Paul Gifford, *Christianity and Politics in Doe's Liberia*, Cambridge, Cambridge U.P., 1993, p.198.

Select Bibliography

Abiodun, Emmanuel, *Celestial Vision of Her Most Rev. Mother Captain Mrs C. Abiodun Emmanuel*, Yaba (Lagos), Charity Press, 4th ed., 1962.

Andersson, Efraim, *Messianic Popular Movements in the Lower Congo*, Studia Ethnographica Upsaliensis XVI, London, 1958.

Assimeng, Max, *Religion and Social Change in West Africa*, Accra, Ghana U.P., 1989.

Assimeng, Max, *Saints and Social Structures*, Tema, Ghana, Ghana Publishing Corporation, 1986.

Baëta, Christian G., *Prophetism in Ghana*, London, SCM Press, 1962.

Barrett, David B., *Schism and Renewal in Africa: An Analysis of Six Thousand Contemporary Religious Movements*, London/Nairobi, Oxford U.P., 1968.

Barrett, David B., *African Initiatives in Religion*, Nairobi, East Africa Press, 1971.

Coker, S.A., *The Rights of Africans to Organize and Establish Indigenous Churches Unattached to and Uncontrolled by Foreign Church Organizations*, Lagos, Tika-Tore Printing Works, 1917.

Daneel, Inus, *Quest for Belonging*, Gweru, Mambo, 1987.

Daneel, Inus, *Fambidzano: Ecumenical Movement of Zimbabwean Independent Churches*, Gweru, Mambo, 1982.

Eternal Sacred Order of Cherubim and Seraphim, *Moses Orimulade*, Ebute Metta (Nigeria), 1962.

Haliburton, G.M., *The Prophet Harris*, London, Longmans, 1971.

Hayward, V.E.W., ed., *African Independent Church Movements*, 1963.

Hollenweger, Walter J., *Pentecostalism: Origins and Developments Worldwide*, Peabody MA, Hendriksen, 1998.

Jules-Rosette, Bennetta, *African Apostles: Ritual and Conversion in the Church of John Maranke*, Ithaca NY, Cornell U.P., York, 1975.

Makhubu, Paulus, *Who Are the Independent Churches?*, Johannesburg, Skotaville, 1988.

Martin, Marie-Louise, *The Biblical Concept of Messianism, and Messianism in Southern Africa*, Morija, Morija Sesuto Book Depot, 1954.

Martin, Marie-Louise, *Kimbangu: An African Prophet and His Church*, Oxford, Blackwell, 1975.

Neufeld, Elmer, *Kimbanguism: An African Prophetic Movement*, Nsukka, University of Nigeria Department of Religion, 1963.

Nussbaum, Stan, ed., *Freedom and Independence*, Nairobi, OAIC, 1994.

Omoyajowo, Joseph Akin, *Cherubim and Seraphim: The History of the African Independent Church*, New York, NOK Publishers, 1982.

Ositelu, J.O., *The Holy Revelation from the Mountain Tabierar for the Year 1951*, Ijebu-Remo, 1951.

Peel, John D.Y., *Aladura: A Religious Movement Among the Yoruba*, London, Oxford U.P., 1968.

Ross, Kenneth, R., ed., *Christianity in Malawi*, Gweru, Mambo, 1996.

Sundkler, Bengt G.M., *Bantu Prophets in South Africa*, London, Oxford U.P., 1st ed. 1948, 2nd ed. 1961.

Sundkler, Bengt G.M., *Zulu Zion and Some Swazi Zionists*, Uppsala, Gleerup, 1976.

Turner, Harold W., *History of an African Independent Church: The Church of the Lord (Aladura)*, 2 vols, London, Oxford U.P., 1967.

Uka, E.M., *Missionary Go Home: A Sociological Interpretation of an African Response to Christian Mission. A Study in Sociology of Knowledge*, Frankfurt-am-Main, Peter Lang, 1989.

Walker, Sheila, *The Religious Revolt in the Ivory Coast*, Chapel Hill, Univ. of North Carolina Press, 1983.

Webster, James B., *African Churches among the Yoruba 1888-1922*, London, Oxford U.P., 1964.

Welbourn, F., *East African Rebels*, London, SCM Press, 1962.

Welbourn, F. and Ogot, B.M., *A Place to Feel at Home*, London, Oxford U.P., 1962.

West, Martin, *Bishops and Prophets in a Black City: African Independent Churches in Soweto*, Johannesburg, David Philip, 1975.

Wilson, B.R., *Sects and Society*, London, Heinemann, 1960.

Wishlade, R.L., *Sectarianism in Southern Nyasaland*, London, Oxford U.P., 1964.